DISCARDED

D1205466

Texas Houses Built by the Book

NUMBER THREE:
Sara and John Lindsey Series in the Arts and Humanities

Texas Houses

Built by the Book

THE USE OF PUBLISHED DESIGNS, 1850–1925

Margaret Culbertson

TEXAS A&M UNIVERSITY PRESS
COLLEGE STATION

Copyright © 1999 by Margaret Culbertson
Manufactured in the United States of America
All rights reserved
First edition

The paper used in this book meets the minimum requirements
of the American National Standard for Permanence
of Paper for Printed Library Materials, z39.48-1984.
Binding materials have been chosen for durability.

Library of Congress Cataloging-in-Publication Data

Culbertson, Margaret.
      Texas houses built by the book : the use of published designs,
1850–1925 / Margaret Culbertson. — 1st ed.
            p.   cm. — (Sara and John Lindsey series in the arts and
humanities ; no. 3)
      Includes bibliographical references and index.
      ISBN 0-89096-863-2 (cloth : alk. paper)
      1. Architecture, Domestic—Texas.   2. Architecture, Mod-
ern—19th century—Texas.   3. Architecture, Modern—20th
century—Texas.
      I. Title.   II. Series.
NA7235. T4C85   1999
728'.09764'09034—dc21   98-42584
                                                                                        CIP

Dedicated to
the designers who shared their work through the printed page
and
the craftsmen who made it a reality

Contents

Illustrations

Acknowledgments

This book would not exist if Ellen Beasley had not been awarded an Architectural History Grant from the Texas Society of Architects in 1980 for a study of the use of design catalogues and other printed sources in Texas communities in the early twentieth century. As a long-time friend, I was intrigued by her original proposal and kept up with the progress she made and the difficulties she encountered. When she left Texas in 1983 to spend a year as a Loeb Fellow at Harvard University, I volunteered to take on the unfinished project. Somehow I never stopped working on the subject, even after completing the original grant report in 1986. Ellen's support and encouragement over the years have been invaluable, as I have continued to study and expand the scope of her original idea.

Many other people and institutions made significant contributions to this book, and the following list is inevitably incomplete. The University of Houston Libraries provided support in many ways, as my employer and as my "home" library, whose Interlibrary Loans Department and Photography Section responded to seemingly endless requests. A 1991 grant from the Art Libraries Society of North America enabled me to examine and index the house designs published in popular and trade magazines of the nineteenth and early twentieth centuries, and the data collected in that study contributed significantly to the research for this book. Drexel Turner and Bruce Webb, as editors of *Cite: The Architecture and Design Review of Houston,* and Mike Hazel, as editor of *Legacies: A History Journal for Dallas and North Central Texas,* gave early encouragement by publishing articles that eventually were expanded to form the basis of this book.

I consulted design sources or supporting historical resources at the following libraries: Avery Architectural and Fine Arts Library at Columbia University, New York City; Boston Public Library; Chicago Public Library; Dallas Public Library; Fondren Library at Rice University, Houston; Houston Public Library; Kansas City Public Library; Library of Congress, Washington, D.C.; Nicholas P. Sims Library, Waxahachie, Texas; Rosenberg Library, Galveston; Texas A&M Library, College Station; University of Houston Libraries; and the University of Texas at Austin Libraries. Many other libraries, particularly the Center for Research Libraries, Chicago, Illinois, made their resources available through interlibrary loans. Staff members of the following Texas libraries, archives, and institutions kindly answered my requests for information about houses in their communities: Bee Public Library in Beeville, Brownwood Public Library, Bryan Public Library, Corpus Christi Public Library, Crockett Public Library, El Paso Public Library, Houston County Historical Commission Archives, First Baptist Church of Bryan, Institute of Texan Cultures, Palestine Public Library, Red River Library in Clarksville, Reeves County Library in Pecos, and Unger Memorial Library in Plainview.

I am grateful to the current homeowners who have provided information, including Byron Black,

LeAnne Davis, John and Glenda Dinyari, Susan Ridgway Garry, and Curtis F. Jeanis. Descendents of original owners were also helpful in the research, including Jeanne Jones Hause, Buddy Hosford, Emily Kemble, and Anne Graham Allen.

Special thanks to Bruce and Barbara Martin, who shared their special knowledge of San Antonio and drove me many miles around the city showing their latest "finds"; to Jeff Fadell and Neal vonHedemann for extensive help with reading and editing the manuscript; to Kaye and Roger Fuller for providing encouragement and a welcoming place to sleep during my Austin research visits; to Michael Tomlan and Michael Alcorn for their help with George Barber information; to Ivon DuPont for sharing his discoveries about Nelson McConnell Irvin; to Gene Crain and Gary Coover for information about the Crain and Williams companies; to Dwayne Jones and the staff of the National Register Division, Texas Historical Commission, Austin, for help with many queries and for allowing me to consult the files in their office; to Shannon Simpson for his help with the resources of the Ellis County Museum; to Carol Roark for alerting me to the R. M. Williamson Collection at the Dallas Public Library; and to Stephen Fox for answering many questions and sharing his issues of *Perspective*. Sims McCutchan provided support in many important ways, including helping me to keep the project in perspective and to take the breaks necessary in order to maintain progress in the long run.

The debt to my parents is too great to describe, but special thanks is given for their unfailing encouragement and support and their invaluable background information about Waxahachie, the town where they grew up and to which they returned to live thirty-five years ago.

Introduction

Of all my magazines, none has given me so much
real pleasure as reading and studying the plans in
American Homes.

—Jane Field Jones

In 1901, Jane Field Jones wrote these words in praise of George F. Barber's magazine of mail-order house designs.[1] The second wife of one of Beeville's most prominent businessmen, Captain A. C. Jones, she was wealthy, well-traveled, and an active counselor in her husband's business affairs (fig. 1).[2] She also was evidently sincere in her praise of Barber's magazine, for when her husband died in 1905, she picked one of Barber's designs from *American Homes* for a new house that she built closer to the town of Beeville than the big country home she had shared with her husband (figs. 2 and 3). Jane Jones would have been well aware of East Coast architectural trends through annual shopping trips to New York City and visits to Saratoga, New York. She could easily have afforded the services of a San Antonio or New York architect, but she chose to build one of George Barber's mail-order designs.[3]

Mrs. Jones was only one of many Texans who utilized house designs published in magazines, books, and catalogues. Homeowners, carpenters, contractors, and even architects took advantage of the unprecedented wealth of published house designs in the nineteenth and early twentieth centuries. This book is intended to increase awareness and understanding of the use of published designs in Texas by providing an introduction to the types of publications that included such designs, as well as by illustrating specific examples of Texas houses based upon them. It also provides a partial social

Fig. 1. Jane Field Jones. Courtesy Jeanne Jones Hause.

Fig. 2. *Jones House, 611 E. Jones St., Beeville, built 1906.* Photo by the author.

Fig. 3. *"Residence on Missionary Ridge, Tenn.," designed by George F. Barber, in* American Homes *3 (Nov., 1896).*

and cultural context for the use of published designs in Texas by presenting background information on some of the owners and builders of these houses.

Few examples of Texas houses based on published designs can be found in previous publications about architectural history or Texas architecture. Historians have long known of the existence of published house-design sources and studied their use and influence, but most drew their examples from areas outside Texas.[4] Texas houses based on published designs have been included in works on Texas architecture, but their derivation from published designs remained unknown and unmentioned until recent years, when a few examples have been included in publications.[5] This book collects previous discoveries and introduces new ones in order to confirm the widespread use of published designs in Texas and to contribute to our understanding of which sources were actually used in the state and who was using them.

The rarity of published Texas examples is, in most cases, probably due to two major factors: the scarcity of documentation and a preference on the part of some people to attribute designs to anonymous, creative carpenter-builders rather than to think of local builders as merely copyists. This preference could derive from any number of influences, including the romantic ideal of the creative individual, and, in the case of mail-order house designs, an association of mail-order catalogues with mass-produced products of bad design or low quality. Whatever the causes, it is hoped that evidence presented in the following chapters will help to reduce any stigma associated with the use of published designs in the nineteenth and early twentieth centuries.

The scarcity of documentation is a factor that has seriously hampered research into the use of published designs in Texas. No sales records of mail-order house-design firms or magazines that sold house designs have survived. Texas carpenters or homeowners may have written about selecting a published design in letters or diaries or kept records that would help provide documentation, but few such records have been discovered. Texans did write testimonial letters to design publishers, and some of the letters were published in magazines or mail-order catalogues, but it takes extensive searching through the design literature of the period, much of which is not easily accessible, to discover these letters.

A few mechanic's liens (contracts between homeowner and builder) named specific published design sources, but most used standardized language that omitted any reference to the source of the designs used. The only way to find the few exceptions is to go page by page through the volumes of mechanic's liens preserved in county records, a process not unlike looking for a needle in multiple haystacks. Visual documentation of Texas houses that match specific published designs can be found, but the process is also slow and often yields no results, since the number of houses and possible designs that could be analyzed is immense.

The examples presented in this book were discovered over a fifteen-year period, primarily through contacts with other researchers and preservationists and through personal research in primary documents. An effort was made to include all areas of the state, but the examples inevitably reflect the vagaries of chance and the cities and towns the author was able to visit and photograph or find illustrated in books, articles, or architectural surveys.[6] Copies of the design sources were collected from reprinted editions and from original editions found in research libraries around the country.[7]

Since the majority of the houses in this book were discovered by visually matching them with published designs, they tend to have distinctive forms or decorative elements that catch the eye and clearly confirm the connection with the printed source. Pattern books, catalogues, and magazines also published many simple, almost generic designs that probably also were used in Texas, but it is far more difficult to identify and prove the use of such designs without some form of corresponding written documentation.

Much remains to be learned about the use of the various design sources, their relative importance, and their place within the broader contexts of domestic architecture and residential development. However, this book shows that numerous examples of the use of published designs in nineteenth- and early-twentieth-century Texas can be found, that many of the resulting houses were outstanding examples of domestic architecture, and that the people who built them included prominent members of the upper middle class, small-scale developers, and middle-class individuals with a wide range of occupations. Even more examples await discovery as people and institutions become more aware of the sources and documents that can assist in the search.

Texas towns, residential neighborhoods, and rural areas have been enriched by houses that were "built by the book." The following chapters introduce the variety of design sources available to Texans in the nineteenth and early twentieth centuries, present a selection of the houses that were built from those sources, and identify some of the people who built them. The book closes with a look at one particular community, Waxahachie, and the place of these houses within the community and in the lives of their owners.

Texas Houses Built by the Book

1

. . . . .

Picking a Pattern

PATTERN BOOKS AND POPULAR MAGAZINES

Ashton Villa looked dramatically different from other Galveston houses when it was completed in 1859. Its ornate cast-iron veranda and distinctive decorative brackets supporting deeply projecting eaves contrasted strongly with the restrained Classical and Greek Revival residences of most of Galveston's wealthy citizens (fig. 6). Although the Victorian fascination with variety and style did not find widespread acceptance in Texas until after the Civil War, a few exceptions to the traditional, rectangular house forms with classical decorative elements began to appear in the 1850s, and Ashton Villa was prominent among them.

The Italianate design upon which Ashton Villa was probably based arrived in Texas on the pages of a women's magazine, *Godey's Lady's Book* (figs. 7 and 8). In the 1840s and 1850s, popular magazines such as *Godey's* began to publish sample designs from a new type of book that was devoted to pre-

senting house designs in a variety of styles. These books, now referred to as pattern books, along with the magazines that published selected designs from them, became the primary means of communicating new architectural developments to Texans during the mid–nineteenth century.

Before American pattern books appeared in the 1840s, builders' guides were the most common type of design publication available to Texans. Asher Benjamin, Owen Biddle, John Haviland, and Minard Lafever authored some of the most popular of the American builders' guides, which were published in multiple editions during the first half of the nineteenth century. These guides provided instruction in the geometrical principles necessary for construction and illustrated the forms and proportions of the various types of classical columns, capitals, and entablatures, known as the orders of architecture. Architectural details, including doorways and window frames, often were illustrated, but very few complete house façades or floor plans were included. The emphasis of the illustrations was on the details that builders could use within traditional house forms.

An example of the probable influence of one of those details is the magnificent front door of the Nichols-Rice-Cherry House (ca. 1850) in Houston, now located in Sam Houston Park (fig. 4). The doorway strongly resembles plate 63 of Lafever's *Modern Builder's Guide* (fig. 5). The curvilinear Greek detailing of the crowning frieze is almost identical to that in Lafever's design, and the recessed door, framed by pilasters, with glass panels above and to the sides, is very close to Lafever's, although these details were considerably simplified.

The details on the outer pilasters, however, are similar to those pictured in a design by Asher Benjamin.[1]

Builders' guides undoubtedly influenced the design of decorative details used in many of the substantial Classical Revival houses of wealthy Texans, such as the Nichols-Rice-Cherry House, but the guides did not constitute a major influence on the basic form and design of most Texas houses in the first half of the nineteenth century.[2] The general public and their carpenter-builders shared a widespread understanding of domestic architecture, in which the basic forms of houses remained fairly constant and relatively simple. Limitations of technology, combined with the difficulty of obtaining building materials during the period, probably

Fig. 4. Entrance Detail, Nichols-Rice-Cherry House, Sam Houston Park, Houston, built ca. 1850. Photo by the author.

Fig. 5. Plate 63, Minard Lafever, Modern Builder's Guide. Courtesy Dover Publications.

contributed to this basically conservative design environment.

Pattern books, and the magazines that helped to popularize them, were important factors in changing this approach to house design. A. J. Downing authored two of the earliest successful American pattern books, *Cottage Residences* (1842) and *Architecture of Country Houses* (1850). His books and those of his followers emphasized designs for complete houses in a variety of styles, rather than details of classical architecture, as earlier builders' manuals had.[3] Early pattern books typically included an exterior view of each house design, along with a floor plan and additional text on such diverse topics as ventilation and landscape design. Also, an introductory text usually emphasized the importance of ownership of well-designed homes to the overall improvement of society and the betterment of mankind. As Downing wrote in his *Cottage Residences* of 1842, "What an unfailing barrier against vice, immorality, and bad habits are those tastes which lead us to embellish a home . . . whose humble roof, whose shady porch, whose verdant lawn and smiling flowers, all breathe forth to us, in true, earnest tones, a domestic feeling that at once purifies the heart, and binds us more closely to our fellow beings."[4] Morality and social improvement undoubtedly provided an intellectual justification for pattern books, but the pleasure of contemplating so many design choices probably also contributed to their success.[5]

Popular magazines, including *Godey's Lady's Book, The American Agriculturist,* and *The Horticulturist* (the latter was edited by Downing himself), encouraged the growing public interest in house designs by featuring selected designs from pattern books and by carrying advertisements for the books as well. Magazines were widely read in early Texas, and the arrival and contents of new issues often were announced in local newspapers.[6] Although the Classical Revival styles predominated in the houses built by prosperous Texans from the 1840s through the early 1860s, a few were built in other styles and demonstrated their owners' awareness of new stylistic developments. Ashton Villa in Galveston and the Erastus S. Perkins Octagon house in Houston both are distinctive pre–Civil War examples of alternatives to the Classical Revival styles that were based on published designs.

The impressive brick residence known as Ashton Villa (2328 Broadway, Galveston) was built in an Italianate style for James and Rebecca Brown in 1859–60 (fig. 6).[7] Rebecca Brown probably was involved in selecting the design for the house, since it is based closely on a design published in the November and December 1858 issues of *Godey's Lady's Book* (figs. 7 and 8). *Godey's,* primarily a fashion and literary magazine for women, was immensely popular in the mid–nineteenth century, with a circulation of 150,000 before the Civil War.[8] The well-to-do and fashionable Rebecca undoubtedly would have seen *Godey's* regularly and easily could have been attracted by the full-page illustration of this house design as she perused the latest illustrations of gowns and bonnets. The likelihood that Rebecca was involved in the selection of the house design is enhanced by the fact that the name "Ashton Villa" came from Rebecca's family. Ashton was Rebecca's middle name, her father's middle name, and the surname of her Revolutionary War ancestor, Lt. Isaac Ashton.

Although the major emphasis of *Godey's Lady's Book* remained fashion and literature, the magazine in the mid-1840s began the practice of publishing an occasional house design along with fashion illustrations, and by the late 1850s a house design was included almost every month. In 1868, publisher Louis Godey reported that more than four thousand cottages and villas had been erected from plans published in his magazine.[9] Most of the designs were selected and reprinted from pattern books published by a variety of architects, until a series "drawn expressly for *Godey's Lady's Book*" by Philadelphia architect Samuel Sloan was begun in

Fig. 7. *House design, in* Godey's Lady's Book *(Nov., 1858).* Reproduction courtesy Houston Metropolitan Research Center, Houston Public Library.

1859.[10] The architect of the 1858 design that attracted the Browns was not named in the magazine, but the style of the drawing and the similarity of the design to others by Samuel Sloan indicate that he was the architect.

The Browns did not copy the *Godey's* design exactly, but they did keep the general massing of the façade, with its slightly projecting central bay, topped by a small pediment; the curved, supporting brackets under the deep eaves; and the delicate filigree of the veranda. The steamy Gulf Coast climate probably was a major factor in their decision to add a second level to the one-story veranda shown in the illustration. They also made changes in the floor plan, particularly by separating the kitchen from the main body of the house, another concession to the climate, and by deleting the projecting bay windows on the sides. The central stair hall and the basic proportions of the flanking rooms remained from the original plan. The final

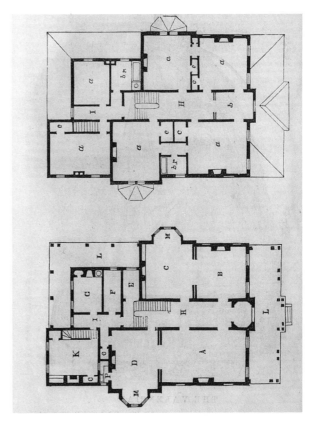

Fig. 8. *Floor Plan, in* Godey's Lady's Book *(Dec., 1858).* Reproduction courtesy Houston Metropolitan Research Center, Houston Public Library.

Fig. 6. *(left) Ashton Villa, 2328 Broadway, Galveston, built 1859–60.* Photo by Ellen Beasley, Houston.

Fig. 9. Erastus Perkins House, Houston, built late 1850s; demolished. From the Wood Map of Houston, *dated 1869.* Courtesy Houston Metropolitan Research Center, Houston Public Library.

result was one of the most stylish, up-to-date, and expensive houses in Texas at the time. Additions and changes have been made to the rear and the east side over the years, but the façade still presents the same composition and Italianate details from the pages of *Godey's* that appealed to the Browns in the late 1850s.

Erastus Perkins was a New Yorker who arrived in Houston in 1838 and built an eight-sided, or octagon, house in the late 1850s or early 1860s (since demolished; see fig. 9).[11] Although Thomas Jefferson designed an octagon house in 1804, the octagonal form was not widely known or used for domestic architecture until Orson Squire Fowler, of New York, began to promote it in the late 1840s.[12] Fowler had made his name in the field of phrenology, the "science" of determining a person's character by feeling the bumps on the skull. But in 1848 he published *A Home for All*, in which he extolled

the benefits and virtues of octagon houses. He claimed that octagon houses were cheaper to build, providing more usable space than an equivalent square or rectangular house, and that they were intrinsically more beautiful than square or rectangular houses, since the octagon was closer to the natural form of the sphere. He revised and reprinted his book several times in the 1850s and also published articles on the subject in such popular magazines as *Godey's Lady's Book*.[13] Authors of popular works on domestic architecture also began to include a few examples of octagon houses in their books, and popular magazines periodically published examples and discussions of the merits of octagonal plans for houses.

Fowler lectured widely to promote his ideas and spoke in Galveston in 1859.[14] Perkins might have heard Fowler lecture or could have read his book, and he also might have been influenced by the octagonal design by Henry A. Page that was published in the magazine *The Horticulturist* in May 1850 (fig. 10).[15] Since Perkins had extensive orchards and vineyards on his Houston property, he well could have subscribed to *The Horticulturist,* which was a periodical directed to gentlemen landowners like Perkins.[16] The article by Page pointed out the advantages of ventilation in an octagon house. Better cross-ventilation was possible through the windows, and, in addition, if the central hall was ventilated through a roof tower, warm air would be drawn up and out through the tower. Both these features were advantageous in Houston's long summers. The details of Perkins's octagon house are hard to distinguish in the woodcut that is the only visual record of his house, but it is clear that he actually built two octagons, one of which was a smaller wing attached to the larger, and that the main octagon did have a roof tower for ventilation, as recommended by Page.

At least two other octagon houses were built in Texas. Chester H. Robbins built one in the late 1850s near Bay City, and W. H. Bridges built the other around 1860 at Meridian. Robbins evidently had read Fowler's book, for his floor plan duplicated one that was labeled as "The Best Plan Yet" in Fowler's *A Home for All.* In Meridian, Bridges built two octagons, as Perkins did in Houston, but Bridges's were essentially two equal-sized octagon rooms joined by a breezeway.[17]

When the Texas economy strengthened after the Civil War and technological developments became more common, more new houses began to reflect the variety of styles being presented in periodicals and pattern books. The unprecedented design variety of the pattern books would not have been possible without the major technological developments of the nineteenth century. Steam-driven saws and presses could cut and mold wood into an endless array of shapes and patterns. The expanding network of railroads could economically carry building materials and decorative details to small

Fig. 10. *"Octagon Villa," designed by Henry A. Page, in* The Horticulturist *4 (May, 1850): frontispiece.* Reproduction courtesy Sterling C. Evans Library, Texas A&M University, College Station.

towns throughout the country. The balloon-frame method of construction, still used in house construction today, permitted the creation of complex, frequently asymmetrical houses that could be built by workers lacking the extensive background and skill that would have been necessary to built such shapes using the older, timber-frame construction methods.

The house built for physician E. S. Look and his family in Clarksville (407 East Main Street) embodies this postwar Victorian delight in variety and ornamentation (fig. 11).[18] It was modeled after a design published by the New York architect E. C. Hussey in his 1875 pattern book, *Home Building* (fig. 12). Hussey described the design as being in the Swiss style and declared, oddly enough, that the "almost excessive frill work gives it a very pretty, although a rather tawdry appearance."[19] The "frill work" was lovingly translated from Hussey's drawing to the three-dimensional form of the Clarksville house, running beneath all the eaves, around the cornice line of the porch, and around the house at the second-floor level; filling the gables; and supporting the deep eaves with decorative brack-

Fig. 11. E. S. Look House, 407 E. Main St., Clarksville, built ca. 1880. Photo by the author.

Fig. 12. Plate 14, E. C. Hussey, Home Building.

ets. Even the use of an iron balustrade over the front porch follows Hussey's recommendation for this design.

Hussey's *Home Building* was intended for the general public, but the plate that inspired the Look House was reprinted three years later in *The Specimen Book of One Hundred Architectural Designs*, a work published by A. J. Bicknell, a New York publisher identified with the production of pattern books for members of the building trade.[20] The *Specimen Book* was a compilation of illustrations from the many pattern books Bicknell published, as well as other works, such as Hussey's, that he handled as a major architectural bookseller. Bicknell's pattern books, as well as the others intended for the building trade and published by George E. Woodward and William T. Comstock, tended to

Fig. 13. John Bremond House, east view, 700 Guadalupe St., Austin, built 1886. Photo by the author.

have more illustrations of architectural details and less text than those intended for the general public.

Bicknell's *Village Builder and Supplement*, published in several editions between 1872 and 1878, evidently influenced the designer of the large two-story house built in Austin (700 Guadalupe Street) for businessman John Bremond in 1886. Ironwork is an important decorative element in this house, as in the Look House, but the larger size of the Bremond house permits an even grander display. The cast-iron porch railings, roof cresting, and finials lend a lacy aspect to this substantial brick and masonry building (figs. 13 and 15). The house was built and probably designed by George Fiegel, who had come to Austin from New Orleans in 1873, at the age of twenty-one.[21] He became a well-respected builder and had constructed other buildings for the Bremond family before undertaking this sizable project. Its finished form, with a full

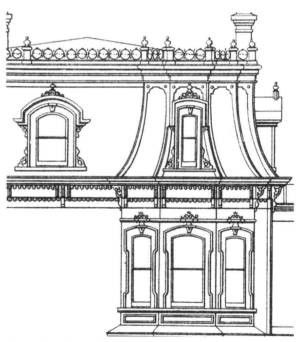

Fig. 14. Detail from Supplementary Plate 2, A. J. Bicknell and Company, Bicknell's Village Builder and Supplement. Courtesy Dover Publications.

Fig. 15. John Bremond House, south view, 700 Guadalupe St., Austin, built 1886. Photo by the author.

Fig. 16. Detail from Supplementary Plate 11, A. J. Bicknell and Company, Bicknell's Village Builder and Supplement. Courtesy Dover Publications.

array of Victorian details, could only have enhanced his reputation. Fiegel seems to have used Bicknell's pattern book as an idea book, selecting individual elements from several different house designs and joining them together in an overall composition very different from the original sources.

The projecting bay with mansard roof on the east side of the house strongly resembles the bay in Supplementary Plate 2 (figs. 13 and 14), while the unusual roof shape sheltering the small window and balcony at the third-floor level of the south side probably was inspired by a similar design in Supplementary Plate 11 (figs. 15 and 16). The decorative shingle pattern of the roof and the masonry band linking the hood moldings of the second-floor windows can be linked to other Bicknell designs.[22]

Fig. 17. Smith M. Ellis House, 422 King William St., San Antonio, built 1888. Photo by the author.

Pattern books for the general public continued to be published along with those for the building trade, and the Philadelphia architect Isaac Hobbs published one entitled *Hobbs's Architecture* that appears to have influenced several Texans. Hobbs, a regular contributor of house designs to *Godey's Lady's Book* between 1859 and 1886, reflected the importance of that publishing venue to his work by dedicating his pattern book "to the many ladies throughout the United States who have for years aided us by their suggestions."[23] Since most of the designs in *Hobbs's Architecture* also were published in *Godey's*, we don't know for sure whether the book or the magazine was the medium through which Hobbs's designs reached the builders of the houses discussed below.

The 1888 Smith M. Ellis House in San Antonio

Fig. 18. Design No. 84, Isaac Hobbs, Hobbs's Architecture, p. 189.

Fig. 19. (above) White Frame House at 710 Houston St., Crockett; demolished. Photo by Todd Webb, safety negative, 1964–1966, P1977.12.172.2, © 1966, Amon Carter Museum, Fort Worth, Texas.

Fig. 20. Design No. 27, Isaac Hobbs, Hobbs's Architecture, p. 75.

FIRST FLOOR.   SECOND FLOOR.

(422 King William Street) repeats the cloverleaf, three-bay façade of Hobbs's Design No. 84 (figs. 17 and 18).[24] Changes in the design include the addition of a second level to the front gallery, probably as a concession to Texas heat, and extending the house to the rear. If the builder originally included the windows emerging from the mansard roof in the Hobbs design, they no longer survive. In the text accompanying the design in his book, Hobbs promised, "Numerous evolutions of this plan can be readily organized by us to suit locality."[25] Whether Ellis requested such changes from Hobbs

Fig. 21. Charles S. House House, Houston, built 1882; demolished. From Art Work of Houston *(Chicago: W. H. Parish Publishing Company, 1894).* Reproduction courtesy Houston Metropolitan Research Center, Houston Public Library.

or whether he asked a San Antonio builder to adapt the original design, the resulting house is a pleasing and cohesive composition of curves and projecting bays that is as distinctive today as when it was built in 1888.

The house that once stood at 710 Houston Street in Crockett probably was inspired by Hobbs's Design No. 27 (figs. 19 and 20).[26] Once again, the design was not copied exactly; the porch was extended, and the slightly projecting part of the façade was switched to the opposite side. However, the distinctive mansard roof and its hooded windows were copied, along with the basic form and plan of the house. The unusual, projecting second-floor bay window, with its turreted roof, may never have been part of the Crockett house, but the first-floor bay window projecting from the parlor on the

Fig. 22. Design No. 1, Isaac Hobbs, Hobbs's Architecture, *p. 23.*

opposite side of the house was included. (The first-floor bay window is on the wrong side of the house to be included in Hobbs's perspective view, but it is clearly shown in his floor plan.)

We do not know who adapted Hobbs's design for the house in Crockett, but we do know that a professional architect adapted another Hobbs design for a house built in Houston (figs. 21 and 22).[27] Architect Eugene T. Heiner in 1882 designed an imposing, towered residence (demolished) for Charles S. House. It repeated many aspects of the Hobbs's design, including the general shape and proportions of the façade, the placement of the tower, the projecting entrance porch with balcony above, the third-floor balcony on the tower, the placement of the windows, and the decorative roof cresting. Whether Heiner routinely consulted pattern books for design ideas or whether Mrs. House asked Heiner to adapt the design from *Godey's,* pattern books were plentiful and an important means for architects to stay abreast of architectural developments in a period when professional architectural publications were few.

The architects who produced pattern books usually justified their publications with purposes similar to those of Isaac Hobbs: "Not only to assist those who may be about to build, but . . . to aid its readers in the cultivation of taste and the love of the beautiful."[28] The architects made sure that their addresses were included in their pattern books, although mail-order commissions were an added benefit, rather than the publications' primary purpose. However, since eager readers did respond to pattern books by requesting copies of specific plans, it was a natural step for architects to move from publishing pattern books to producing mail-order catalogues for the specific purpose of selling plans. The resulting publications are the subject of the next chapter.

2

. . . . .

Victorian Variety

MAIL-ORDER HOUSE CATALOGUES AND MAGAZINES

*The plans . . . for your house are progressing finely
and [we] think you will be very much pleased with them.
We will ship to you next week.*

—*Palliser, Palliser and Co., New York,
to T. Gonzales, Galveston*

In 1886, after a major Galveston fire destroyed his family's home, Thomas Gonzales, a prominent cotton buyer, ordered plans for a new house by mail from an architectural firm in New York City. That firm, Palliser, Palliser and Co., was a leader in the new practice of using mail-order catalogues to sell house designs throughout the country. These catalogues presented page after page of designs in a format very similar to that of pattern books: exterior view and floor plan, accompanied by brief textual descriptions. However, catalogues such as the Pallisers' possessed the added feature of an invitation to the reader to order detailed plans and specifications by mail. Although the Pallisers were not the first to offer house plans for sale by mail, they were the first firm to find widespread and continuing success in doing so, and their success enticed many competitors into the field.

Catalogues of mail-order house plans merged the presentation and the design variety of pattern books with the commercialism of the nation's growing consumer culture. By the late nineteenth century, such catalogues had become a major force in the creation of domestic architecture in Texas and the rest of the United States. Some catalogues even began to offer, in addition to plans, all the building materials for a house, pre-cut to the appropriate sizes. The catalogues that offered only plans became known as "plan books," probably to distinguish them from the pre-cut or ready-cut house catalogues. However, since the term "plan book" is no longer common, the more descriptive term "house catalogue" will be used here to refer to catalogues selling plans, and the term "ready-cut house catalogues" will refer to catalogues selling building components for entire houses.

The development of mail-order house catalogues began in the 1850s, when a few pattern books included brief announcements of the availability of more detailed plans for purchase. One of the earliest of these, *Village and Farm Cottages,* published in 1856 by the architectural firm of Cleaveland and Backus, was similar in format and approach to the pattern books by Andrew Jackson Downing, but with the significant variation of a "Notice" page, printed directly after the preface, which stated: "For the convenience of such as may wish to build any of the designs in this work, the Authors have prepared careful, lithographed working drawings and printed specifications for each. These comprise every thing necessary to enable any competent workman fully to understand the plans."[1] Prices ranged from three to five dollars, depending on the complexity of the design.

Occasional offers to sell detailed plans continued to appear in a few pattern books and magazines during the 1860s and early 1870s, but the practice did not become widespread until after 1876, when George Palliser, then in Bridgeport, Connecticut, published his first catalogue, *Palliser's Model Homes for the People.*[2] It was a small booklet of forty-four pages, selling for twenty-five cents. A second, more elaborate catalogue, *Palliser's American Cottage Homes,* was published in 1878, by which time George's brother Charles had become a partner in the firm. The brothers moved to New York City in 1883, where they continued to produce catalogues, and from which they wrote to Mr. Gonzales in Galveston in June 1886 that the plans for his house were "progressing finely" and would be shipped the next week.[3] Gonzales bought a large piece of property on the outskirts of town and shifted the old house that was on the property to make room for his new house. However, in the end, Gonzales and his family renovated the old house and moved into it, never actually building from the Palliser plans that they had bought.[4]

A Palliser design that did get built in Texas was the James M. Cotton House, erected in Houston in 1882 (figs. 23 and 24). Although Houston architect George Dickey included the Cotton House in a list of his own work, a visual comparison of a surviving photograph of the Cotton House with the Palliser design shows that much was owed to the Pallisers.[5] The Cotton family may have brought the Palliser catalogue to Dickey and asked him to adjust the design to their needs, or Dickey could have kept a variety of house catalogues in his office for clients to consult and use in defining their design preferences. The latter arrangement may have been the case, given the fact that another house designed by Dickey, the Charles Dillingham House, built in Houston in 1889, also was based very closely on a design published in a house catalogue (fig. 25).

The catalogue design upon which the Dillingham House was modeled was published by the Pallisers' first major competitor, Robert W. Shoppell (fig. 26).[6] Unlike the Pallisers, Shoppell had a background in publishing rather than architecture. However, he recognized a good marketing idea in house catalogues and started producing his own in the early 1880s. He then began the first mail-order architectural periodical, *Shoppell's Modern Houses,* in 1886. The designs he published he credited to a group of architects called the Cooperative Building Plan Association. Although the exterior of the Dillingham House was clearly based on Shoppell's Design No. 485, once again Dickey was listed as the architect in local sources.[7] Since neither the house nor the floor plans survive, we do not know whether Dickey altered the interior plan or used the Shoppell plan as published.

As the Dillingham House and the Cotton House indicate, it was not unusual for an architect to consult house catalogues for design ideas, but it probably was more common for carpenter-builders, contractors, and members of the general public to actually order plans from house catalogues, as well as to use them for ideas. Shoppell was particularly assiduous in collecting and publishing testimoni-

Fig. 23. *James M. Cotton House, Houston, built 1882; demolished.* Courtesy Houston Metropolitan Research Center, Houston Public Library.

als from satisfied customers, and these letters give us an indication of the range of Texans who ordered house plans from catalogues, although in most cases their houses have not survived to show us the designs they chose. Cliff A. Adams, mayor of Bryan from 1889 to 1900; William M. Robinson, a dealer in agricultural implements in Dallas; and George L. Price, a bank teller in Houston, all wrote letters to Shoppell in 1889, expressing satisfaction with his plans. In other years, Shoppell also published the names of residents of Denison, El Paso, Galveston, Laredo, Paris, and Plano as satisfied customers. Builders from El Paso and Laredo were listed as approving the reliability of his plans and specifications.[8]

Shoppell was only the first of the Pallisers' many competitors in the house-catalogue business. The

Fig. 24. *"View of F. Egge's Cottage," in* Palliser's Model Homes.

Fig. 25. Charles Dillingham House, Houston, built 1889; demolished. Courtesy Houston Metropolitan Research Center, Houston Public Library.

Fig. 26. Design No. 485, Shoppell's Modern Houses *2 (Aug., 1887): 18.*

American public began to order plans in greater numbers, and their choices multiplied as more designers and publishers entered the field. House catalogues were advertised in popular periodicals, including *Ladies' Home Journal* and *American Agriculturist*, as well as in periodicals for the building trade, such as *Carpentry and Building* and *Builder and Woodworker.* The catalogues usually sold for fifty cents to a dollar and illustrated from fifty to one hundred designs in each edition. The catalogue producers often repeated their own designs from earlier editions, but widespread copying of designs from other catalogues did not occur until the early years of the 1900s. Even so, most early catalogues were copyrighted and occasionally carried warnings similar to the one used by D. S.

Hopkins in his 1889 catalogue: "The publisher of this work is protected by the Copyright Laws of the United States, and hereby warns all persons that no plan or portion of plan represented herein may be copied or used without permission of the publisher."[9]

People liked and used house catalogues for several reasons. Catalogues offered consumers far more choices in home designs than had ever been available before. The variety of plans within each catalogue was frequently emphasized in advertising, on the cover, and within the introduction or preface. The catalogues also offered security in dealing with contractors and builders. As the introduction in an 1895 catalogue stated, "Our aim is to so construct and word our plans . . . so there can be no misunderstanding between builder and owner."[10]

House catalogues also presented their houses as being more stylish and embodying better design than those that might be available from local builders. In addition to all these advantages of good design, variety, and security, the catalogues offered the always powerful incentive of saving money. It was cheaper and easier to order plans from a catalogue than to commission a custom design from an architect.

House catalogues even helped to democratize domestic architecture by putting a wide variety of design choices directly into the hands of the consumer. Of course, the actual choices were closely related to developments in technology and related changes in the manufacturing and distribution of building materials, but all of these factors combined to provide middle-class Americans with more choices than they had ever had before. The residential neighborhoods constructed during this period reflect this new freedom.

Herbert Chivers of Saint Louis took the consumer appeal of variety seriously when he started publishing larger and larger editions of his catalogue, *Artistic Homes*. An advertisement from 1901 proclaimed a new edition, "double its former size," that contained 800 designs. The 1903 edition con-

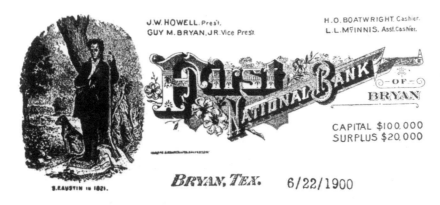

Fig. 27. Letter from L. L. McInnis, printed in Herbert C. Chivers, Artistic Homes, *p. 837. Reproduction courtesy Fondren Library, Rice University, Houston.*

Fig. 28. 730 N. Main St., Cleburne. Photo by the author.

Fig. 29. "Thornburg Residence," designed by Herbert C. Chivers, in Herbert C. Chivers, Artistic Homes, *p. 416. Reproduction courtesy Fondren Library, Rice University, Houston.*

tained 995 designs, and by 1910 Chivers was advertising a thousand-page catalogue with over 1500 plans.[11] His catalogues also often included reproductions of letters from satisfied customers. R. D. Gage, first county attorney for Reeves County and president of the Pecos Valley Bank, wrote a letter praising the plans he had ordered for his house in Pecos (421 S. Willow) in 1902; the house still survives, although with alterations. Additional Texas clients who wrote letters to Chivers included L. L. McInnis, assistant cashier of the First National Bank in Bryan; J. W. Butler, a banker in Clinton; and B. N. Leonard in Baird (fig. 27).[12] Houses similar to a Chivers design entitled "Thornburg" were built in Fort Worth (demolished) and Cleburne (730 N. Main; figs. 28 and 29).[13]

The democratization of the mail-order approach applied to the producers of house catalogues as well as their consumers. The medium could even be used to advantage by a woman trying to establish a practice in a male-dominated profession. Mr. and Mrs. W. T. Stewart of Corsicana probably would have been surprised to learn that the E. E. Holman, from whom they ordered plans for their 1907 house, actually was a woman.[14] Emily Elizabeth Holman practiced architecture in Philadelphia from 1893 to 1914.[15] She published several house catalogues and advertised them extensively in the *Ladies' Home Journal* and *House Beautiful,* but always using only her first initials (fig. 30).

In a slightly later period, another woman also marketed her designs through house catalogues, but without using the ambiguity of initials. Leila Ross Wilburn of Atlanta, Georgia, published at least nine catalogues, beginning in 1914.[16]

Another aspect of this democratization of domestic architecture through house catalogues is indicated by the places where the catalogues were produced. Many came from the traditional East Coast publishing and design centers of New York and Boston, but such disparate cities as Chicago, Illinois; Grand Rapids, Michigan; and Carthage, Illinois, also were homes to thriving catalogue businesses. An energetic entrepreneur, regardless of his location, could use mail-order distribution channels to establish a successful practice with the potential to influence domestic architecture throughout the United States and beyond.

A few house catalogues were even produced in Texas. In 1910, a Dallas-based organization, Associated Architects, published *Fifty House Plans Designed for Home Builders in the Southwest.* The catalogue was advertised in the *Dallas Morning News,* with a selling price of fifty cents.[17] The introduction to the catalogue emphasized that the designs of the Associated Architects were especially appropriate for the Southwest due to such features as "wide airy porches, cool inviting halls and balconies, and the number and proportion of win-

IF you want Beautiful Complete House Designs, send
for my Books.
Book of Bungalows, by mail . . . $2.00
Picturesque Summer Cottages . . $1.00
Picturesque Suburban Houses . . $2.00
E. E. HOLMAN, Espen Building, Philadelphia, Pa.

Fig. 30. Advertisement for E. E. Holman's catalogues, in Ladies' Home Journal *27 (Apr., 1910). Reproduction courtesy Houston Public Library.*

Fig. 31. 4719 Swiss Ave., Dallas, built ca. 1910. Photo by the author.

Fig. 32. Plan No. 48, Associated Architects, Fifty House Plans for Home Builders in the Southwest, *p. 56.*

dows."[18] Many of the designs illustrated in the catalogue exactly match houses in the Dallas development of Munger Place. Since several of these houses predate the 1910 catalogue, it is possible that they actually were the original houses photographed for the catalogue. One of the finest of these is the two-story neoclassical house at 4719 Swiss Avenue, which matches Plan No. 48 (figs. 31 and 32). The house at 4935 Victor has been altered but still strongly resembles No. 48 as well. The distinctive house with Craftsman-style details at 5007 Victor (figs. 33 and 34) exactly matches Plan No. 18, and the house at 5022 Rieger is very similar to the same plan. As the descriptive text in the catalogue for this design stated, "Greater individuality than shown here could hardly be wished for."[19] The house at 5019 Tremont, also in Munger Place, matches Plan No. 28 (figs. 35 and 36).

Fig. 33. 5007 Victor St., Dallas, built ca. 1910. Photo by the author.

The individual names of the Associated Architects are not given in their house catalogue; they are described simply as being "among the foremost men of the profession."[20] The Dallas city directories do give the names of the managers: Irving A. Walker in 1910 and Joseph O. Thompson from 1911 through 1915. Since Thompson was listed independently as an architect in the 1916 directory, it is possible that some of the designs were his.

Other Texas producers of house catalogues include the Dallas firm of Ye Planry and the Houston-based T. J. Williams House Manufacturing Company and Crain Ready-Cut House Company, discussed in chapters 5 and 6.

Although George F. Barber's catalogues were produced in Tennessee rather than Texas, this self-trained architect probably was the most popular

Fig. 34. Plan No. 18, Associated Architects, Fifty House Plans for Home Builders in the Southwest, *p. 26.*

Fig. 35. E. C. Moore House, 5019 Tremont St., Dallas, built 1909. Photo by the author.

Fig. 36. Plan No. 24, Associated Architects, Fifty House Plans for Home Builders in the Southwest, *p. 32.*

of the house-catalogue architects in Texas in the late nineteenth and early twentieth centuries. Since so many Texas houses were based on his designs, chapter 3 is devoted to them.

3

· · · · ·

Mail-Order Master

GEORGE F. BARBER

*I have the best house in North Texas, and this seems to be
the verdict of all who have seen it.*

—*S. L. Erwin, Honey Grove*

Merchant S. L. Erwin wrote those proud words about his new house in Honey Grove, built in 1896 from plans created by house-catalogue architect George F. Barber, when the house was featured in Barber's magazine, *American Homes* (fig. 37).[1] Mr.

Erwin's house, unfortunately, no longer stands, but the T. W. Trout House (705 Poplar), of obvious Barber inspiration, does survive in Honey Grove, serving as a tangible reminder of the mail-order architect's influence in the town (figs. 42 and 43).[2] However, Honey Grove was not unique in benefiting from Barber's designs. Houses based on the work of this talented and prolific architect were built all over Texas—in large cities, in small towns, and on remote farms and ranches. As an example, a single design was built in at least three totally different settings across the state: on a Central Texas farm south of Hutto (later moved to a site near Coupland), in the coastal port town of Orange (803 N. Sixth Street), and on the plains of

*Fig. 37. S. L. Erwin House, Honey Grove, built 1896, demolished.
American Homes 4 (Feb., 1897): 37.*

Fig. 38. Saul-Garry House, built 1905–1906, originally located south of Hutto, later moved to this location in the country near Coupland. Photo by the author.

Fig. 39. Holland House, 803 N. Sixth St., Orange, built ca. 1910. Photo by the author.

Fig. 40. J. N. Donohoo House, Plainview, built ca. 1907; moved to
unknown location. Postcard, ca. 1910. Private collection.

West Texas in the town of Plainview (moved to
unknown location; see figs. 38, 39, 40, and 41).[3]

The man who spread his works so liberally
throughout Texas and the rest of the United States
never received any formal architectural education
(fig. 44).[4] Born in De Kalb, Illinois, in 1854 and
raised on a farm near Marmaton, Kansas, Barber
taught himself the basics of architectural design by
studying handbooks, pattern books, house catalogues, and journals that he ordered by mail.[5] He
learned the practical aspects of building construction while working as a carpenter. Although he
tried his hand as a dealer in nursery stock in 1878,
he continued both to work at least part-time as a
carpenter and to teach himself architecture. By 1884
he had moved back to De Kalb to work for his older
brother's contracting and building firm and soon
was acting as its architect. Thus, at the age of thirty,
Barber finally had reached the point where he could
begin to make a name for himself as an architect.
Evidently he was determined that his success would
reach the wider world in some of the same published forms from which he had learned—
journals and house catalogues.

Barber began his publication campaign by submitting copies of his designs to architecture and
building journals and also by sending them notices

of his design and building activities. He found
some success in this approach, for a few of his notices were published in the news summaries of *The
Inland Architect* in 1887 and 1888, and two of his
house designs were published in *Carpentry and
Building* in 1888.[6] He was to find more success,
however, in publishing his own house catalogues.
Even while he was submitting material to journals,
he must have been assembling a collection of designs for a catalogue.

Barber's first catalogue did not look like a book
or even a booklet. It consisted of eighteen designs
printed on cards (6¾ by 5¼ inches) that were tied
together at the corner with yarn. The first card bore
the impressive title *The Cottage Souvenir: Eighteen
Engravings of Houses Ranging in Price from $900.00
to $8,000.00 in Wood, Brick and Stone, Artistically
Combined.* A few months later, in 1888, he produced a catalogue of fifty-six pages, stapled together, *Modern Artistic Cottages; or the Cottage Souvenir, Designed to Meet the Wants of Mechanics and
Home Builders.* It sold for eighty-five cents and
invited the reader to correspond with the author
in order to obtain detailed plans and specifications.
Even though they were modest in size, these two
catalogues provided a foundation for the growth
of Barber's business and reputation.

In 1888, the same year that he published his second catalogue, Barber moved to Knoxville, Tennes-

Fig. 41. Design No. 263, George F. Barber, Modern Dwellings,
3d ed., p. 317.

Fig. 42. T. W. Trout House, 705 Poplar, Honey Grove, built 1895. Photo by the author.

Fig. 43. "In North Carolina Mountains," designed by George F. Barber, in American Homes *5 (July, 1897): 8.*

see. The notice that he sent to *Carpentry and Building* regarding the move gave his health as the reason, but he also may have felt that Knoxville would be a more suitable base for his publishing ventures.[7] During the next two years, Barber worked at establishing his practice in Knoxville, while he also traveled and worked in the Midwest and the South.[8] He continued to accumulate examples of his designs, and in 1889 he published another portfolio of designs on cards, which he sold for eighty-five cents.[9]

Finally, in 1891, Barber produced a full-blown catalogue, his 168-page *Cottage Souvenir No. 2: A Repository of Artistic Cottage Architecture and Miscellaneous Designs,* which contained designs for fifty-nine houses, as well as carriage houses, two churches, two stores, and three gazebos, which Barber referred to as "summer houses" (fig. 45).

Fig. 44. Portrait of George F. Barber. American Homes 2 *(Jan., 1896).*

"cottage" soon was replaced by the more up-to-date "modern" and "artistic" in the titles, with *Artistic Homes* and *Modern Dwellings* each being published in several editions. Barber advertised his catalogues widely in national magazines, including *Ladies' Home Journal* and *Scribner's,* meeting with such success that by 1900 his firm was the largest architectural office in Knoxville, with clients all across the United States and as far away as Japan and South Africa.[11]

That the *Cottage Souvenir No. 2* and its "revised and enlarged" edition of 1892 were used in Texas is without doubt. Texas houses based on the designs abound. The house in Ladonia (603 E. Bonham Street) built in 1894 for merchant J. B. Haden and his wife Elizabeth and the house in Athens (demolished), built in the mid-1890s for Charlie Coleman, both duplicated Design No. 1 (figs. 46 and 47).[12]

In addition to the wide-ranging use of its de-

Fig. 45. Title page of George F. Barber, Cottage Souvenir No. 2 *(1891).*

Barber also included designs for a selection of interior and exterior details, including wall cabinets and gable ornaments. Plans and working drawings were available for all of the designs, ranging in price from two dollars for the gable ornaments to sixty dollars for an elaborate two-and-a-half-story wood and brick residence with a tower. Texas was represented in the catalogue with a photographic illustration of the staircase and hall of a house in Beaumont, built by the Reliance Lumber Company for its president, William Weiss.[10]

The *Cottage Souvenir No. 2* was phenomenally successful, and Barber followed it with a new edition the next year, *The Cottage Souvenir, Revised and Enlarged.* He continued to produce catalogues almost yearly for the next sixteen years. The term

Fig. 46. Haden House, 603 E. Bonham St., Ladonia, built 1894. Photo by the author.

signs by individual Texans such as the Hadens and the Colemans, the *Cottage Souvenir No. 2* seems also to have been used by the developers of Houston Heights in building houses for themselves and their early clients. Of nine houses presented in woodcuts on a Heights promotional brochure of the 1890s, five are based on designs from the *Cottage Souvenir No. 2.*[13] In fact, some of the woodcuts probably were drawn from the plates of the catalogue rather than the actual houses, for vegetation and shadows duplicate those found in Barber's illustrations (figs. 47 and 48). Two of the Barber houses on the brochure are still standing,

Fig. 47. (right) Design No. 1, George F. Barber, Cottage Souvenir No. 2 *(reprint, 1982).*

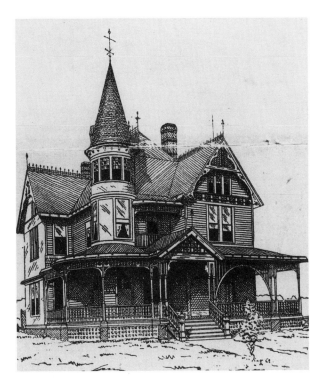

Fig. 48. House on Heights Boulevard, Houston, from Map of Houston Heights, *n.d. Courtesy Special Collections and Archives, University of Houston Libraries.*

the Milroy House at 1102 Heights Boulevard and the Mansfield House at 1802 Harvard (figs. 49, 50, and 51).

Another factor contributing to Barber's success after the *Cottage Souvenir No. 2* was a publishing venture that he initiated in January 1895. The magazine *American Homes: A Journal Devoted to Planning, Building and Beautifying the Home* probably was modeled after *Shoppell's Modern Houses,* the magazine of another mail-order architectural firm (see chapter 4), but Barber's publication was much closer to being a genuine "home magazine" than Shoppell's was. Barber's house designs were featured, and advertisements for his catalogues were prominent, but the work of other architects occasionally was presented, and verse and fiction accompanied articles on such diverse subjects as interior decorating, gardening, and the history of architecture.

Like Jane Field Jones, whom we met in the introduction to this book, many Texans subscribed to *American Homes* and ordered plans from Barber. W. H. Thompson of Georgetown and a "Mrs. B. P." of Weatherford wrote letters of praise to Barber that were quoted in the magazine, along with the one from Mrs. Jones.[14] Photographs of three Texas houses designed by Barber were featured in *American Homes.* The exterior of the Barthold House in Weatherford was published in the September 1895 issue, and two photographs of its interior were included in the August 1896 issue.[15] A full-page photograph of the Erwin house in Honey Grove graced the title page of the February 1897 issue (fig. 37); and the substantial, brick Jester house in Tyler was presented in the October 1898 issue (fig. 52).

The February 1901 issue of *American Homes* featured a design for a cottage that Barber titled "On a Texan Prairie" (fig. 53). He did not publish the location or the owner's name, although the K. D. Lawrence House in Lovelady (Noble Street) is very similar, except for the small gabled balcony at the peak of its roof that is missing from the *American Homes* design but does appear in a similar design published in the same issue and in another version of the design in a 1902 catalogue (fig 54).[16] The text that accompanies the "Texan Prairie" design in the magazine suggests that Barber may have visited Texas at least once in the course of his business. It begins: "If you have never enjoyed the wide sense of freedom experienced by the prairie dweller, particularly on the Texas prairies, you ought to go down there and spend a—well, maybe you would stay. This cottage was designed for just such a person, who went down from the North and couldn't find it in his heart to leave."[17]

Although the term "cottage" is in the titles of all of Barber's early catalogues, most of the houses pictured within are far more elaborate than the modest dwellings we now associate with that term. Even in the nineteenth century, his larger, two-

Fig. 50. Milroy House, 1102 Heights Blvd., Houston, built ca. 1896. Photo by the author.

Fig. 49. Design No. 30, George F. Barber, Cottage Souvenir No. 2 *(reprint, 1982), p. 66.*

Fig. 51. Mansfield House, 1802 Harvard, Houston, built 1896. Photo by the author.

Fig. 52. Jester House, 630 S. Fannin, Tyler, built ca. 1898. George F. Barber, Modern Dwellings, 3d ed.

story houses seldom would have been called cottages.[18] However, the term had been popularized by Andrew Jackson Downing in his pattern books of the mid–nineteenth century, and the later publishers of house catalogues continued to use the term for its association with desirable, tasteful, and fashionable dwellings. The Pallisers titled their 1877 catalogue *Palliser's American Cottage Homes,* and in 1886 the Michigan architect David S. Hopkins titled his first catalogue *The Cottage Portfolio.* Barber was following these successful predecessors when he decided to use the term "cottage" in the titles of his first catalogues. His later use of the terms "modern" and "artistic" in catalogue titles and advertisements was designed to appeal to the same market with more up-to-date terminology.

During twenty years of active production, Barber and his employees and partners produced hundreds of designs in a wide range of styles and sizes and probably sold more than twenty thousand sets of plans.[19] Since many of the designs were published in several editions of the catalogues and often were repeated in the magazine *American Homes* as well, it is impossible in most cases to specify the exact catalogue or issue that served as the design source for a particular house. However, the designs in these pages clearly are the sources of these Texas houses, even if they were ordered, or borrowed, from a different edition of a catalogue or issue of *American Homes* than the one from which our illustration was obtained.

Most of Barber's early designs consisted of eclectic interpretations and combinations of late-Victorian styles, and Design No. 53 from the *Cottage Souvenir No. 2* is an excellent example in a predominantly Queen Anne style that was built in more than one Texas town (fig. 55). Crockett merchant J. E. Downes and his wife Elizabeth selected it for their new house in 1891 (206 N. 7th Street) (fig. 56), and E. A. Blount in Nacogdoches (demolished) also used it.[20] The distinctive onion-domed tower and two triangular-gabled dormers also appear in the Stark house in Orange (611 W. Green Avenue), which was completed in 1894.[21] The exterior design elements that identify Barber's design as Queen Anne include elaborate spindlework decorating the porches and gables, asymmetrical façade, corner tower, steeply pitched roof with front-facing gable, and shingles on the tower and beneath the eaves, contrasting with horizontal wood siding.

Design No. 56—built in Waxahachie, Weatherford, and, in an enlarged variation, in Houston Heights—also displays the characteristic Queen Anne elements of elaborate spindlework, asymmetrical façade, steeply pitched roof with front-facing gable, and shingle siding contrasting with clapboards (figs. 57, 58, and 59).[22] The tower is placed in the center of the façade, rather than on the side, but its unusual interruption of the front gable negates any hint of symmetry that the central position might have suggested.

Barber's 1892 catalogue, *The Cottage Souvenir, Revised and Enlarged,* featured his Design No. 27, which was built in Calvert (609 Gregg) (figs. 60 and 61).[23] Once again, Queen Anne elements predominate, although the masonry corner chimney, with its round-arched window, displays Romanesque Revival characteristics.

Barber had a definite flair for grouping and bal-

Fig. 54. K. D. Lawrence House, Noble St., Lovelady, built ca. 1899. Photo by the author.

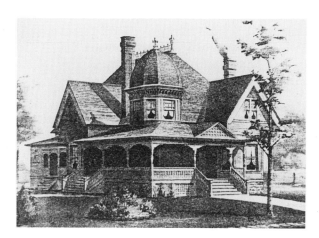

Fig. 53. "On a Texan Prairie," designed by George F. Barber, in
American Homes *12 (Feb., 1901): 81.*

ancing the "gingerbread" elements of late-Victorian eclectic styles, but he also kept up with new stylistic developments in domestic architecture, developed his own interpretations, and added them to his catalogues. He first included new "Colonial" designs in his 1893 catalogue, *New Model Dwellings and How Best to Build Them.* Many of the designs referred to as "Colonial" in the late nineteenth and early twentieth centuries essentially applied Colonial details to houses with Queen Anne form and massing.

A design in the January 1896 issue of *American Homes* was one of Barber's designs in the new Colonial style, although from today's vantage point

Fig. 56. J. E. Downes House, 206 N. 7th St., Crockett, built 1891–93. Photo by the author.

it does not appear particularly Colonial. Its gambrel-roofed dormers, classical porch columns, and the balustrade above the central entrance porch were strong indications of its Colonial identity during Barber's time. These "up-to-date" Colonial elements appealed to the builders of the Lambertson House in Brownwood (611 Coggin Avenue) and the Waddell House in Houston (demolished) (figs. 62, 63, and 64).[24]

"Classic Colonial" was the term used by Barber to describe Design No. 1 in his 1901 *Modern Dwellings* catalogue, but today it would be classified as a Neoclassical, rather than Colonial, design, due to

Fig. 55. Design No. 53, George F. Barber, Cottage Souvenir No. 2 *(reprint, 1982), p. 113.*

Fig. 57. Design No. 56, George F. Barber, Cottage Souvenir No. 2 (reprint, 1982), p. 119.

Fig. 58. F. P. Powell House, originally located on the northwest corner of W. Marvin at Bryson St., Waxahachie, built 1892; demolished. Courtesy Ellis County Museum, Waxahachie.

Fig. 59. Mills House, Heights Blvd., Houston, built 1893; demolished. From Art Work of Houston (Chicago: W. H. Parish Publishing Co., 1894). Reproduction courtesy Houston Metropolitan Research Center, Houston Public Library.

HOW TO BUILD
ARTISTIC HOMES

Plans and designs for the interior and exterior of
Beautiful Homes, ranging in cost from $500 to $18,000.

A Text Book of Modern Architecture

brimful of beautiful illustrations and home-building knowledge,
together with designs for laying out and beautifying your grounds.
Sent for ten cents in postage or silver, if you mention this paper.
GEO. F. BARBER & CO., Architects, Knoxville, Tenn.

Fig. 60. Design No. 27, by George F. Barber, as reproduced in an advertisement in Ladies' Home Journal *10 (May, 1893). Reproduction courtesy Houston Public Library.*

Fig. 61. Parish-Jones House, 609 Gregg, Calvert, built 1898. Photo by the author.

its two-story portico supported by classical columns. Houses based on this design were built in Houston and Bryan, but unfortunately both have been demolished (figs. 65 and 66).[25]

Barber also demonstrated his awareness of new architectural developments when he included an early bungalow design, which he titled "Rustic," in his 1902–1903 catalogue, *Art in Architecture* (fig. 67). Houston artist George Westfall must have appreciated the design's new and "artistic" elements, for

AMERICAN HOMES.   3

Fig. 62. *"Artistic Colonial Home," in* American Homes 2 *(Jan., 1896): 3.*

Fig. 64. *Waddell House, 2404 Caroline St., Houston, built ca. 1901; demolished. From* Art Work of Houston *(Chicago: W. H. Parish Publishing Company, 1894).* Reproduction courtesy Houston Metropolitan Research Center, Houston Public Library.

Fig. 63. *Lambertson House, 611 Coggin Ave., Brownwood, built ca. 1901.* Photo by the author.

Fig. 65. Design No. 1, George F. Barber, Modern Dwellings, 3d ed., p. 104.

he chose it for his new home on Hawthorne Street in 1905 (fig. 68).[26] The overall simplicity of the design; its low, spreading roof with overhanging eaves; and the rustic stone porch and chimney all stood in dramatic contrast to most of the other designs in Barber's catalogues and to most domestic architecture in Texas at the time. The design definitely was a harbinger of the bungalow craze that soon would transform the residential neighborhoods of the nation. Although Barber produced several bungalow designs in later catalogues, he never adopted the style wholeheartedly, and his catalogues began to lose their popularity as catalogues of bungalow designs from California began to proliferate after 1906 (see chapter 5).

Fig. 66. Hackney House, 2210 Main St., Houston, built 1903; demolished. Courtesy Houston Metropolitan Research Center, Houston Public Library.

Barber continued his local Knoxville architectural practice even after he published his last catalogue in 1907. His son, Charles Ives Barber, joined the firm in 1910, after studying architecture at the University of Pennsylvania. When Barber died in 1915, only a week after the death of his wife, his service was held in the newly completed Christian Church designed by his son.[27]

George F. Barber, self-taught architect though he was, probably was the most popular of the mail-order architects whose catalogues reached Texas. Only a small fraction of the Texas houses based on his designs have been illustrated here. Many of the favorite surviving Victorian houses in Texas towns can be traced to Barber designs, and elements from those houses and designs then were borrowed and used by Texas builders in a multitude of related

Fig. 67. "Rustic" Design 580, George F. Barber, Art in Architecture, *2d ed., p. 185.*

Fig. 68. Westfall House, 393 Hawthorne St., Houston, built 1905. Photo by the author.

Fig. 69. 619 7½ St., Houston, built 1996. Photo by the author.

houses. More than a hundred years after they were created, Barber's designs are being adapted and used again for contemporary construction (fig. 69). Barber's architectural legacy in Texas has reached into every corner of the state and continues to provide visual interest and pleasure to Texans.

4

. . . . .

Myriad of Magazines

HOUSE DESIGNS IN MAGAZINES AFTER THE CIVIL WAR

To build, erect and complete an aero-bungalow, frame dwelling house,
consisting of eight rooms and one gallery . . . as per plat in
Holland's Magazine, *Nov. 1921 issue, page 37.*

—*Mechanic's Lien, Navarro County*

When J. W. Harris and his wife Tillie specified this *Holland's Magazine* design in the contract with their builder for a new house in Blooming Grove, they were following in the footsteps of many earlier Texans by finding their dream home within the pages of a magazine (figs. 95 and 96).[1] After the Civil War, popular magazines flourished and provided house designs to many Texas readers receptive to the new styles and forms. Women's magazines and agricultural magazines continued to publish house designs, and soon they were joined by magazines produced for the building trades, magazines produced for the primary purpose of selling house designs and plans, and popular magazines devoted to all aspects of the home.[2] A few Texas magazines also published house designs, and many Texans evidently liked their emphasis on the work of regional architects and on designs appropriate for the local climate, as Tillie and J. W. Harris liked the

bungalow they selected from the pages of the Dallas-based *Holland's*.

Women's magazines multiplied after the Civil War, and *Godey's Lady's Book* faced powerful new competitors in such publications as *Woman's Home Companion*—originally titled *Ladies' Home Companion* when it was created in 1873—and *Ladies' Home Journal*, begun in 1883. During this period, *Godey's* continued to provide house designs to its readers, along with fashion and fiction, and architect Isaac Hobbs was the primary architect featured. In February 1880, the magazine illustrated a house in San Diego, Texas, designed by Hobbs for N. G. Collins, a member of the Texas Legislature.[3] This "Gothic Cottage," as it was titled, possessed a T-shaped floor plan with three verandas on different sides of the house, perhaps a response to the South Texas climate. Its "Gothic" elements included steep gables, patterned shingle roof, and filigree

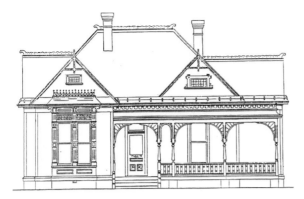

Fig. 70. "A Southern Cottage," designed by J. M. Archer, in
National Builder 16 (Apr., 1893): 78. Reproduction courtesy
Center for Research Libraries.

ornamentation on the gables and the verandas.
Hobbs's designs reached many Texans through his
pattern books, as well as through *Godey's Lady's
Book;* and houses in San Antonio, Crockett, and
Houston derived from his designs are discussed in
chapter 1.

New magazines created for the building trades
provided carpenters and contractors with information on technological developments and house
designs. Builders found such designs helpful in
meeting the expectations of their clients, who
wanted new houses like those they were seeing in
magazines and catalogues and in their own towns
and neighborhoods. Among the more successful
and enduring of these magazines were *American
Builder and Journal of Art* (begun in 1868), *Manufacturer and Builder* (1869), *Carpentry and Building* (1879), *National Builder* (1885), and *Scientific
American, Architects and Builders Edition* (1885). All
of them provided detailed house designs and plans,
along with other practical information and instruction. Since the designs in builders' magazines
were intended for practitioners, more illustrations
and details were included than in pattern books.
Many builders' magazines also encouraged readers to submit their own plans for publication, often offering cash prizes in design competitions.

In response to a call for inexpensive cottage

plans by *National Builder* in 1892, J. M. Archer submitted a design for a frame, one-story cottage that
he had built in Abilene (fig. 70). *National Builder*
published Archer's design, along with his letter, in
which he indicated that the same house was being
duplicated in Baird, Texas.[4] The design is representative of many Texas cottages of the period, in
which a basic square form with pyramidal roof is
elaborated by pushing forward a room with bay
window and gable roof on one side of the façade
and balancing it with a decorated front porch that
continues around the other front corner of the
cottage. The decorative woodwork, or gingerbread,
is most prevalent on the front gables, bay window,
and porch.

In 1899, *National Builder* published the design
for another Texas cottage, this one designed by
F. W. Langworthy and built in Waco (fig. 71). It was
the featured plan of the issue and thus included a
variety of detailed drawings on a fold-out sheet, as
well as a list of materials used in the construction
and estimated costs. The accompanying text
praised the design, stating that it was "especially
adapted to meet the requirements of a southern
home." The same magazine published another cottage design built in Waco by Langworthy in the
January 1902 issue.[5]

A design published in *Carpentry and Building*
in 1888 seems to have inspired the builder of the

Fig. 71. "Waco House," designed by F. W. Langworthy, in
National Builder 29 (Dec., 1899): 8.

Fig. 72. Clendenen House, front view, 803 N. Main St., Bonham, built ca. 1888. Photo by the author.

Albert J. Clendenen House in Bonham (803 N. Main Street; figs. 72, 73, and 74).[6] The design was an early work by George F. Barber, submitted to the magazine before he had published any house catalogues, when he was still living in De Kalb, Illinois. The Bonham builder substituted a gable roof for the shed roof over the second-floor porch and added another second-floor porch above the bay window on the south side, but his debt to Barber is evident.

Scientific American, Architects and Builders Edition was an impressive publication, presenting eight to ten house designs in each issue and including color as well as black-and-white plates, on large-format pages. It originally was intended for the building trades, but soon the publishers began

marketing it to the general public as well, and its many high-quality illustrations helped to expand its readership. Advertisements for the magazine were placed in popular magazines, as well as local newspapers, to help boost circulation. The *Beaumont Enterprise* was one of the Texas newspapers that carried these advertisements in 1889.[7]

The advertisements must have convinced at least some Texans to subscribe to *Scientific American, Architects and Builders Edition,* for Connecticut architect Joseph W. Northrup's elaborate, turreted Queen Anne design, published in the May 1892 issue, can be found in Waxahachie, where it was built for the Patrick family (figs. 148 and 149); and the smaller Colonial Revival design by Edwy

Fig. 73. Clendenen House, side view. Photo by the author.

E. Benedict, published in the September 1901 issue, was duplicated in Houston (figs. 75 and 76).[8] The Houston example was built around 1908 in the streetcar suburb of Woodland Heights and was owned first by Joseph E. Anderau and his wife, Alma. Anderau had immigrated from Switzerland in 1898, at the age of twenty-four, but by the time he moved into his new house on Bayland, he was working as chief engineer of the Savoy Apartments, an exclusive apartment house on Main Street in downtown Houston.[9]

Although it never was the magazine's primary purpose, for a period in the 1890s *Scientific American, Architects and Builders Edition,* did offer to sell detailed plans and specifications for its house designs, following the example of other magazines that were created for that purpose, particularly *Shoppell's Modern Houses. Shoppell's,* founded in 1886 by

Fig. 74. "Residence of W. G. Earle," designed by George F. Barber, in Carpentry and Building *10 (Nov., 1888): plate 43.*

Fig. 75. *Anderau House, 405 Bayland, Houston, built ca. 1908.* Photo by the author.

Fig. 76. *"Dwelling at Waterbury, Conn.," designed by Edwy E. Benedict, in* Scientific American, Architects' and Builders' Edition *32 (Sept., 1901): 49.*

house-catalogue publisher Robert W. Shoppell, probably was the first successful magazine created to sell house plans. In addition to reprinting designs from his house catalogues in the magazine, Shoppell printed articles on home-related topics, including furnishings, the use of color in interiors, and landscape gardening. Since almost all the designs published in the magazine also were included in the firm's mail-order catalogues, it is impossible to know whether the catalogues or the magazine inspired specific houses. However, houses that duplicate Shoppell's designs have survived (figs. 25 and 140), indicating that, in one form or another, Shoppell's publications made their way to Texas.

Shoppell's success with his magazine inspired other mail-order architects to publish their own magazines. George F. Barber initiated the magazine *American Homes* in 1895 (see chapter 3), and Min-

Fig. 77. 1348 Heights Blvd., Houston. Photo by the author.

neapolis architect Walter J. Keith began his magazine, originally titled *The Homebuilder,* in 1899. After his own *American Homes* ceased publication in 1904, Barber started submitting designs to Keith's publication, whose title had changed in 1901 to *Keith's Magazine on Home Building.* One of Barber's designs, published in the September 1906 issue and titled "A Compact Modern House" (figs. 77 and 78), was built on the main boulevard of the Houston Heights (1348 Heights Boulevard).[10] Barber's design brings variety and interest to a simple foursquare house by chamfering the corners of the parlor at the front of the first floor and cutting back the second-floor area above the entrance porch in order to insert a tiny bay-windowed sewing room. However, the second-floor bedroom façade, projecting above the parlor and beside the sewing room, seems uncomfortably flat and plain in contrast to the rest of the façade.

Fig. 78. Design A181 by Barber & Klutz, Architects, in Keith's Magazine on Home Building *16 (Sept., 1906): 162.*

Unlike Shoppell's, Keith's, and other mail-order house-plan magazines, *The Craftsman* during its early years actually offered to send subscribers free detailed plans for its house designs.[11] Gustav Stickley started the magazine in 1901 to promote the Arts and Crafts movement in the United States. The format, paper, and printing of the magazine, reflecting the Arts and Crafts design aesthetic, were of higher quality than those of most popular magazines of the period. The decorative arts were always a major component of the magazine, but, beginning in 1903, house designs also were featured regularly. Stickley was an early proponent of bungalows, and in *The Craftsman* he published designs for, and articles about, bungalows and other houses embodying his principles of good construction and simplicity of design and materials. These Arts and Crafts designs, in short, were the antithesis of the complex, elaborate, decorated houses so popular in the late nineteenth century and presented in so many popular magazines and house catalogues.

A good example of Craftsman simplicity of design is the house built for Vila and Julian C. Harris in Fort Worth in 1912, modeled on a design first published in the July 1909 issue of *The Craftsman* and reprinted in the 1912 book *More Craftsman Homes* (figs. 79 and 80).[12] Harris, who worked as a bookkeeper for the Cobb Brick Company, substituted clinker brick for the stone in the original design, but the brick's rough texture and variations in color achieved an effect comparable to that of rough-hewn stone. The house embodies the Craftsman principles of simplicity of design and use of appropriate materials. The texture and color of the bricks, along with the mass and shape of the house, are its defining elements, not the use of columns, brackets, or other applied decoration.

Simplicity also characterizes the house built for Fred J. Feldman of El Paso (1105 Prospect), although the dark wood of the window frames, set against the light stucco of the second floor, creates a contrasting effect and geometric pattern very different from the monolithic mass of the Harris House (figs. 81 and 82).[13] Feldman took a Craftsman plan first published in July 1905 and had his builder, E. Kneezel, modify and enlarge it in a manner that evidently met with Stickley's approval, since the El Paso house was featured in the October 1911 issue of *The Craftsman.* The article on the house emphasized that "no unnecessary ornament, useless fretwork or idle decoration mars the solid worth of it."[14]

Theodore S. Smith, who worked for the San Antonio Printing Company, probably was representative of many Texans in his admiration of *The Craftsman* and its house designs. He was a young man twenty-four years of age when he wrote a letter that was published in a 1905 issue of the magazine. In addition to stating that *The Craftsman* was, "without exception, the best magazine on the market," Smith indicated his approval of its house designs and plans: "It is said that a kingdom has been offered for a horse, a soul for youth, but neither of these appeal to me like a Craftsman home. I hardly know when I will be able to build a home, but I will never be contented until I own one built on the Craftsman plan."[15]

Texas magazine editors could not ignore the growing popular interest in house designs and inevitably followed the lead of national publications by including house designs. The Texas Farm and Ranch Publishing Company of Dallas first ventured into publishing house designs in its magazine *Farm and Ranch.* The "Residence of Moderate Cost," published in the January 5, 1901, issue, was the first in a series of "practical Southern homes," designed by the Dallas architect E. H. Silven, that continued for two years. According to notes at the end of the design descriptions, each house actually had been built in the city of Dallas. Thanks to the exposure in *Farm and Ranch*, they were built across the state of Texas as well. The magazine did not sell plans, but interested readers were encouraged to contact the architect directly.

Fig. 79. Harris House, 4621 Foard St., Fort Worth, built 1913. Photo by Byrd Williams.

Surviving examples of Dallas houses matching *Farm and Ranch* designs include 2902 Swiss Avenue (figs. 83 and 84) and 2906 Swiss Avenue.[16] A particularly pleasing example of Silven's interest in decorative dormers and gables is the design published in the issue of February 9, 1901. Houses based on this design can be found in Plano (1813 K Street), Hubbard (500 Magnolia Street), and Marlin (505 Williams Street; see figs. 85, 86, 87, and 88).[17]

In 1905, Texas Farm and Ranch Publishing Company took over the publication of *Street's Weekly* and changed its frequency to monthly and its title to *Holland's Magazine* (Frank P. Holland was president of the company).[18] As a general-interest magazine with an emphasis on the home, *Holland's* reached a much broader segment of the population in the Southwest than *Farm and Ranch*

Fig. 80. "Craftsman Stone House with Practical Built-In Fittings" (Craftsman House No. 71), in The Craftsman 16 (July, 1909); reprinted in Gustav Stickley, More Craftsman Homes, p. 70. Reproduction courtesy University of Houston Libraries.

Fig. 81. Feldman House, 1105 Prospect, El Paso, built ca. 1910, in The Craftsman 21 (Oct., 1911): 85. Reproduction courtesy Houston Metropolitan Research Center, Houston Public Library.

Fig. 82. "Craftsman House: Series of 1905, Number VII," in The Craftsman 8 (July, 1905). Reproduction courtesy Houston Metropolitan Research Center, Houston Public Library.

and proved to be a more suitable magazine for publishing house designs. Such designs were a frequent feature in the magazine from 1905 until well beyond 1930. Beginning in 1918, plans for the featured houses could be ordered from the magazine for prices ranging from ten to twenty-five dollars. The magazine probably obtained many of the plans that it sold from a local firm with the memorable name Ye Planry, for all the designers and authors credited in the magazine during this period were either employees or officers of Ye Planry. The architects who provided designs for *Holland's* were based in Dallas or Fort Worth and included W. G. E. Rolaff, W. H. Keyser, J. E. Bridgman, and R. E. Sutherland.

The majority of designs presented in *Holland's*

Fig. 83. Arnold House, 2902 Swiss Ave., Dallas, built 1901. Photo by the author.

Magazine were for middle-class dwellings in a variety of sizes and styles. The editors avoided the tendency of many magazines to publish grand mansions and concentrated on modest but pleasing designs that were more likely to be built by their readers. A design presented in the May 1920 issue of *Holland's* was built at least twice in Fort Worth, at 2812 Avenue D and 2228 Harrison; and twice in San Antonio, at 1102 W. Magnolia and 1115 W. Craig (figs. 89, 90, and 91).[19] However, since the same design, with its rhythmic, repeating gable rooflines, was included in a 1916 Ye Planry advertisement,[20] we do not know for sure whether these builders selected their plans from *Holland's* or a Ye Planry plan book.

Plan No. 2522, published in the June 1920 issue of *Holland's*, and the Texas houses that echo it, demonstrate another situation where it is difficult

Fig. 84. "Cottage of Moderate Cost," by E. H. Silven, in Farm and Ranch *20 (Nov. 16, 1901): 13. From the collection of the Texas/Dallas History and Archives Division, Dallas Public Library.*

to make definitive attributions to *Holland's* when no documentary evidence has survived. Plan No. 2522 is a two-story stucco house with a porte-cochere in a clean, modern style strongly influenced by Frank Lloyd Wright (fig. 92).[21] L. T. Dernier, who was associated with the Dallas firm Ye Planry, was credited with the design. Texas houses that match it can be found in Wichita Falls (2009 Huff Street), Kerens (340 S. Throckmorton Street), and San Antonio (1206 W. Russell) (fig. 93). These houses might have been based on the design published in *Holland's,* or they might have been built from a Ye Planry plan book. The same design, identified as a "Ye Planry Home," was featured in the *San Antonio Light* in 1921. It is also possible that at least one of the owners selected the design from *Keith's Magazine on Home Building,* which featured the same two-story stucco house design in its

Fig. 85. "Modern Southern Cottage," by E. H. Silven, in Farm and Ranch *20 (Feb. 9, 1901): 18.* From the collection of the Texas/Dallas History and Archives Division, Dallas Public Library.

Fig. 86. 1813 K St., Plano. Photo by the author.

Fig. 87. 500 Magnolia St., Hubbard. Photo by the author.

Fig. 88. 505 Williams St., Marlin. Photo by the author.

Fig. 89. Plan No. 2007, in Holland's Magazine (May, 1920): 24.
Reproduction courtesy Houston Public Library.

Fig. 90. 2228 Harrison St., Fort Worth. Photo by the author.

Fig. 91. 1115 W. Craig, San Antonio. Photo by the author.

Fig. 92. Plan No. 2522, in Holland's Magazine *(June, 1920): 22.* From the collection of the Texas/Dallas History and Archives Division, Dallas Public Library.

Fig. 93. 1206 W. Russell, San Antonio. Photo by the author.

December 1916 issue (fig. 94). *Keith's* titled the design "A Well-Planned and Attractive Stucco House" and credited A. S. Barnes as the architect. Barnes happens to have been the president of the original Los Angeles Ye Planry.[22]

Unlike the previous visual matches, the design source of the Harris House in Blooming Grove (617 Fordyce) is unequivocal, since the contract with the builder specifically stated that the house should be built according to a design published in *Holland's Magazine* (figs. 95 and 96).[23] Visually, the house does not resemble its model as closely as the previous examples do, for the more steeply pitched

Fig. 94. "A Well-Planned and Attractive Stucco House," designed by A. S. Barnes, in Keith's Magazine on Home Building 36 *(Dec. 1916): 385.* Reproduction courtesy Houston Public Library.

Fig. 95. J. W. Harris House, 617 Fordyce, Blooming Grove, built 1922. Photo by the author.

Fig. 96. "Plan No. 1," in Holland's Magazine *(Nov., 1918): 37.* From the collection of the Texas/Dallas History and Archives Division, Dallas Public Library.

roof, the use of wood siding rather than stucco, and the later alteration of the front porch change the appearance of the house. The floor plan, however, was copied exactly from the magazine onto the contract. The house is a compact, straightforward example of an airplane bungalow, or "aero-bungalow," as stated in the contract, which means that it is essentially a one-story house with a sleeping room perched on the spreading roof like the cockpit of an airplane over its wings.

Bungalows had become the standard form for small houses by the early 1920s, when the Harrises built theirs, and the numbers that were built dramatically changed the look of many towns and neighborhoods. Magazines and house catalogues were major factors in familiarizing the public with the new form and in disseminating bungalow designs. Our next chapter will investigate Texas bungalows and their design sources.

5
. . . . .
Bungalows from Books

MAIL-ORDER BUNGALOW CATALOGUES

*Your bungalow book came O.K. and I am
very much interested with many of the plans
as I knew I would be.*

—Glen W. Herrick, College Station

When he wrote those words in May 1909, Herrick, state entomologist and a professor at Texas A&M University, was praising the copy of Henry L. Wilson's *Bungalow Book* that he had ordered for the price of one dollar (fig. 97).[1] Wilson's was one of many mail-order catalogues of bungalow designs that emerged after 1905 in response to a growing popular fascination with bungalows (fig. 98). The alliterative title that Wilson picked for his book became the common term for this type of catalogue, "bungalow book." Herrick left Texas before building his Wilson bungalow, but Richard T. Bibb's bungalow in Fort Worth (at 1816 Hurley) appears to have been based on one of Wilson's designs (figs. 99 and 100).[2]

Although the word "bungalow" originally came from India via England, the American bungalow, as developed in the early 1900s in California, looked distinctly different from the Indian huts and the

English cottages first designated by the term.[3] The American bungalow typically was a small house of one or one-and-a-half stories, with wide overhanging eaves, often with decorative rafters or brackets supporting them, and broad porches. The

Fig. 97. Cover of Henry L. Wilson, The Bungalow Book.

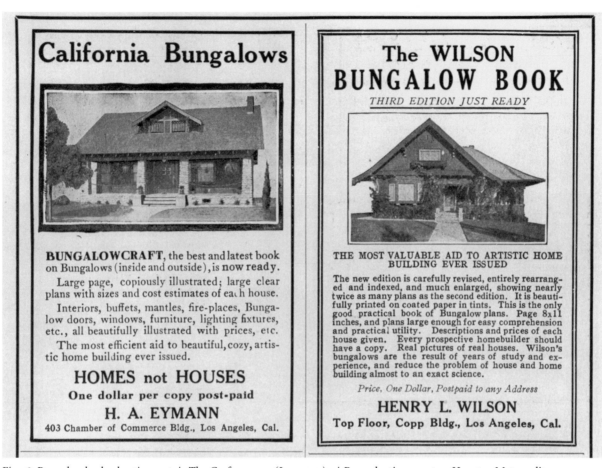

California Bungalows

BUNGALOWCRAFT, the best and latest book on Bungalows (inside and outside), is now ready.

Large page, copiously illustrated; large clear plans with sizes and cost estimates of each house.

Interiors, buffets, mantles, fire-places, Bungalow doors, windows, furniture, lighting fixtures, etc., all beautifully illustrated with prices, etc.

The most efficient aid to beautiful, cozy, artistic home building ever issued.

HOMES not HOUSES

One dollar per copy post-paid

H. A. EYMANN

403 Chamber of Commerce Bldg., Los Angeles, Cal.

The WILSON BUNGALOW BOOK

THIRD EDITION JUST READY

THE MOST VALUABLE AID TO ARTISTIC HOME BUILDING EVER ISSUED

The new edition is carefully revised, entirely rearranged and indexed, and much enlarged, showing nearly twice as many plans as the second edition. It is beautifully printed on coated paper in tints. This is the only good practical book of Bungalow plans. Page 8x11 inches, and plans large enough for easy comprehension and practical utility. Descriptions and prices of each house given. Every prospective homebuilder should have a copy. Real pictures of real houses. Wilson's bungalows are the result of years of study and experience, and reduce the problem of house and home building almost to an exact science.

Price, One Dollar, Postpaid to any Address

HENRY L. WILSON

Top Floor, Copp Bldg., Los Angeles, Cal.

Fig. 98. Bungalow book advertisements in The Craftsman 15 *(Jan., 1909): vi.* Reproduction courtesy Houston Metropolitan Research Center, Houston Public Library.

overall proportions were more horizontal than the bungalow's nineteenth-century predecessor, the cottage. This horizontal emphasis was accomplished by building bungalows closer to the ground than cottages and by making the pitch of bungalow roofs lower. Even though the word *bungalow,* like *cottage,* implied a small house, bungalow books included designs for large, two-story houses using decorative elements common to bungalows, and such houses were built in bungalow developments as well.

The American public, aided and abetted by the popular media, fell in love with this new house type. Bungalows represented the fresh, informal, healthful approach to living typical of their California birthplace. They were inexpensive to build,

they were stylish, and it was easy to get plans for them. Bungalow designs began to appear in popular magazines and house catalogues around 1900 and continued to adorn their pages well into the 1920s. Entire books dedicated to designs of the new house type, the aforementioned bungalow books, appeared around 1906.[4] A full set of plans and specifications ordered from a bungalow book usually cost only ten dollars, and retail lumber yards even offered some free as a way to sell their lumber.

There was a great deal of "borrowing" of designs among bungalow book producers, with many of the same designs appearing in the catalogues of completely different firms, a practice that makes definite attribution of built houses to specific catalogue sources problematical. However, proof that

Fig. 99. R. T. Bibb House, 1816 Hurley St., Fort Worth, built ca. 1912. Photo by the author.

Fig. 100. Design No. 357, Henry L. Wilson, The Bungalow Book, p. 66.

certain sources actually were used can be found in a few builders' contracts and also in testimonial letters that were published in bungalow books. Visual matches of houses with published designs can also indicate the use of specific designs, even if the exact catalogue that was used cannot be verified. E. W. Stillwell was unusual among bungalow book producers in admitting that not all of the houses pictured in his books had been designed in his office and gave the following as a positive explanation for the situation: "We have combed the country for the very best designs and have increased the variety of our offerings by including some of these with our own. For those designs not originated by us we have made new, and we believe, better interior floor plans."[5] However, like most bungalow book publishers, he did not credit other designers in his books, and he probably did not compensate them either.

The overhanging eaves and broad porches of bungalows were ideal for the heat of Texas summers, and Texans welcomed the economical but stylish designs offered in bungalow books. Glenn Herrick left College Station before he could build his bungalow home, but thousands of other Texans caught the bungalow bug. The heroine of Anne Fellows Johnston's 1910 novel, *Mary Ware in Texas*, shared this attraction to bungalows, and her thoughts and comments express the appeal that bungalows held for Texans of that time. In the novel, when she must search San Antonio for a house to rent for her family, Mary has a "vision of a charming little bungalow . . . half hidden in vines." In the Laurel Heights neighborhood, she finds a bungalow closely resembling the one of her dreams, a newly constructed five-room bungalow with a number of attractive features, which she lists: "The electric lights, the convenient little bathroom, the open fire-place in the living room, the built-in china closet." Her brother loves the "good, wide porches to hang a hammock on."[6] As these passages indicate, the modern conveniences that usually were included within bungalows formed a major part of their appeal, but just as important were the design elements that fostered the bungalow's image of closeness to nature: its wide porches, low foundations, and pergolas or attached trellises to support the sheltering vines that were so important in Mary Ware's idyllic vision.

Wilson's *Bungalow Book* was only one of many design sources available to home builders such as Glenn Herrick and Mary Ware's potential landlord. Bungalow books were advertised in popular, home-oriented magazines, including *Ladies' Home Journal, House Beautiful,* and *The Craftsman,* and they could be ordered for one dollar or less. The cost of the book usually would be deducted from the price of any plans selected.

Contractors often were willing to work from bungalow book illustrations, without ordering the detailed plans, but publishers were quick to point out the dangers of this threat to their profits. The Dallas firm Ye Planry warned in its 1914 bungalow book, *Beautiful Homes:*

> The greatest mistake so often made by home builders is to allow the contractor to build your home without prepared plans and specifications. It is too much like making a dress without a pattern. You will save the cost of the plans many times over in your saving on material and labor. The plans and specifications are self-explanatory and eliminates [sic] every possible unnecessary personal controversy between yourself and [the] contractor and between laborers.[7]

Even with such warnings, many homebuilders took the bungalow books directly to their contractors, but enough people ordered the detailed plans to keep plenty of bungalow book publishers in business.

Houstonian J. L. Jones was among the Texans who supported E. W. Stillwell by ordering several bungalow plans in 1913 and 1914. The owner of a furniture store in downtown Houston, Jones bought three empty lots in the small Westover Addition west of downtown Houston in 1913 and 1914, and constructed three houses to sell, using plans ordered from a catalogue published by E. W. Stillwell of Los Angeles. After completing the first house, he wrote the following letter to Stillwell: "I am more than pleased with the house. The floor plan is exceedingly good and the outside is very pretty. It is entirely different from the general run of bungalows you see here. . . . The foreman told me the plans worked out better than any ordered plans he had ever handled. . . . I have two more houses to build, and would like to order more plans from you."[8]

J. L. Jones sold his three houses in April and May 1914, and one of them, a modest bungalow at 1112

Fig. 101. 1112 W. Drew, Houston, built 1914. Photo by the author.

Fig. 102. Design No. W-948, E. W. Stillwell, West Coast Bungalows, *p. 48.*

West Drew, survives and matches Stillwell's Design No. W-948 (figs. 101 and 102).[9]

Tyler physician L. E. Smith and his wife Isabel had a local architect, R. H. Downing, prepare plans for a design they selected from Standard Building Investment Company's *Standard Bungalows,* and in 1922 they contracted with a local builder to construct their bungalow (434 S. Chilton).[10] It still stands today and looks very much like its catalogue design source (figs. 103 and 104). The most obvious external design changes were the use of standard bricks, rather than the rough clinker bricks shown in the catalogue, and the change in the window arrangement on the second floor, which now is partially obscured by the addition of an awning. The small second-floor bedroom is what identifies the house as an airplane bungalow, or "aero-

Fig. 103. *L. E. Smith House, 434 S. Chilton, Tyler, built 1922.* Photo by the author.

Fig. 104. *Design No. 801, Standard Building Investment Company,* Standard Bungalows, *p. 36.*

Fig. 105. 904 Ave. A, Santa Anna. Photo by the author.

Fig. 106. Design No. R-911, E. W. Stillwell, Representative California Homes, *p. 11.*

bungalow," as they were sometimes called. The second-floor room perches on the spreading roof like the cockpit of an early airplane over its wings. Airplanes were an exciting new technological achievement when bungalows were being built, and the use of the term for this type of bungalow associated it with the latest developments.

Another airplane bungalow with bungalow-book inspiration was built in Santa Anna (904 Avenue A; see figs. 105 and 106). It appears to be based on E. W. Stillwell's Design No. R-911.[11] As in the Smiths' bungalow, the repetitive front-facing gable roofs are an important design component.

A more flamboyant airplane bungalow in San Antonio (834 Iowa Street), first owned by physician Charles A. Whittier and his wife Augusta, seems to have been inspired by Design No. 634 of

Fig. 107. C. A. Whittier House, 834 Iowa St., San Antonio, built ca. 1925. Photo by the author.

Seattle architect Jud Yoho (figs. 107 and 108).[12] In his 1916 bungalow book, *Craftsman Bungalows*, Yoho described the design's curved rafters and brackets as "derived from the architecture of Japan and China."[13] The curved Oriental elements were kept in the San Antonio bungalow, but the porch piers were reduced in size, and the second-floor balcony was left out. The plan was also reversed, in response to the corner site.

In addition to such one- and one-and-one-half-story bungalows, Texans also liked the full two-story designs that could be found in bungalow books. Such houses cannot be classified as bungalows, but they were included in bungalow books, and they did incorporate many of the same decorative elements used in bungalows, including broad porches and overhanging eaves with deco-

Fig. 108. Design No. 634, Jud Yoho, Craftsman Bungalows, p. 8.

Fig. 109. G. S. Berry House, 1404 S. Adams St., Fort Worth, built 1907. Photo by the author.

Fig. 110. Design No. 118, Henry L. Wilson, The Bungalow Book, p. 14.

rative rafters or brackets. A two-story design from Henry L. Wilson's *Bungalow Book,* Design No. 118, served as a model for the first residence to be constructed in a small Fort Worth subdivision (1404 S. Adams Street; see figs. 109 and 110).[14] One of the developers, John W. Broad, had lived on the West Coast from 1896 to 1906 and might have picked up a preference for the new style or even acquired an early edition of Wilson's *Bungalow Book* while he was there. This design emphasizes the upper part of the house by concentrating decorative woodwork and brackets on the small projecting window at the attic level and the triangular gables above the second-floor bay windows.

One of the most popular of the designs built in Texas from Wilson's *Bungalow Book* was also for a two-story house, Design No. 397. A well-preserved example of the design is located in the Houston neighborhood of Woodland Heights (429 Bayland; see figs. 111 and 112), but it was also built in Dallas (705 12th Street) and Beaumont (1531 Liberty).[15] In this design, Wilson disguised a basic square house by putting a gable roof over the entrance porch and moving it to one side of the façade, placing a projecting second-floor bay on the other side; varying the window patterns; and, most dramatically, inserting the sweeping, curved, asymmetrical front-gable roof. Henry W. Horton and his wife Maggie were the first owners of the Woodland Heights house, which was built in 1908 and was one of the first houses on the main avenue of the development. Horton, a jeweler with a store on Main Street in downtown Houston, lived in the house with his wife and his youngest son Earl, who worked part-time in the jewelry store. According

Fig. 111. Design No. 397, Henry L. Wilson, The Bungalow Book, p. 92.

Fig. 112. Horton House, 429 Bayland, Houston, built ca. 1908. Photo by the author.

to the census of 1910, the Hortons also took in two boarders, a thirty-two-year-old physician and a forty-year-old druggist, to fill the rooms of their new house and help with expenses.[16]

Developers found bungalow books useful in their efforts to create new neighborhoods that would appeal to a rapidly expanding middle class. Woodland Heights in Houston, the site of Henry Horton's house, provides an example of how bungalow books influenced the appearance of one particular development in the early years of the twentieth century.

The development of Woodland Heights began in 1907 as a project of the William A. Wilson Realty Company (William A. was no relation to Henry L. of bungalow-book fame). It was a streetcar suburb of six hundred building lots, located less than two miles northwest of downtown Houston, on the north side of White Oak Bayou. Since the elevation of the land was ten feet higher than that of downtown, and since there were some trees remaining in what had been an area of small produce farms and woods, the name Woodland Heights was not totally fanciful. The developers also planted numerous live oak and sycamore trees that grew beautifully over the years to justify the neighborhood's name.[17]

Like many developers of the period, the Wilson Realty Company did not supply all of the house designs that were built in Woodland Heights; many purchasers of lots used their own contractors and designs. However, of those houses illustrated in various promotional publications as being built by the company, most of the bungalow designs can be traced to bungalow books of the period. Details and floor plans may have been altered by the company's draftsmen, but the design influence is clear.

The John J. Bruce house (3215 Morrison) was modeled on Design No. R-951 in Henry Stillwell's *Representative California Homes,* a popular bungalow book of the period (figs. 114 and 115).[18] Bruce

was a cement contractor who advertised in the Wilson Realty promotional publications and probably did work in their developments. He and his wife had no children, but they took in as boarders a couple with a ten-year-old daughter, according to the 1910 census. The design of the house, with its gambrel-roofed entrance porch, was distinctive and was used at least two other times in Wilson developments, once more in Woodland Heights (1400 block of Wrightwood, demolished), and in a scaled-down version in Eastwood (4524 Rusk), the 215-acre development east of downtown Houston that the Wilson Realty Company initiated in 1911. (The design also shows up in San Antonio [1115 West Magnolia Street], in a development of the same period [fig. 113].)

Stillwell's designs were not the only ones to appear in Woodland Heights. Henry L. Wilson's *Bungalow Book,* in addition to providing the design of the Henry Horton House, probably inspired the bungalows built at 3302 Beauchamp, 3301 Houston Avenue, and 3301 Morrison. The house at 3302 Beauchamp, first owned by Mrs. Jennie Saunders, was described as a "beautiful bungalow home" in a 1910 promotional brochure (figs. 116 and 117). The gable-roofed, central dormer and wide front porch repeat Wilson's straightforward bungalow design. Wilson's Design No. 394, with its central shed-roof dormer and porch, forty feet wide with brick pilasters, inspired the house at 3301 Morrison, first owned by Alfred E. Ward and his wife (figs. 118 and 119). Ward, an Englishman who had immigrated in 1880 when he was fifteen, managed an armature works. The oldest of his three daughters, aged twenty in 1910, worked as a stenographer in a lawyer's office. (This same design was built by the Wilson Realty Company at 4002 Austin, south of downtown.)[19]

The "charming five-room bungalow" at 3301 Houston Avenue in Woodland Heights repeats Wilson's Design No. 357, with its large bay window, geometric porch balustrade, and ornamented

Fig. 113. 1115 W. Magnolia St., San Antonio. Photo by the author.

porch gable, even though the width of the porch was reduced (figs. 120 and 100).[20] The pattern of the decorative timbers beneath the porch gable varies only in the reversed placement of the two curving timbers. Each of its five rooms must have been fairly full in its early years, for six people were living in the house when the census takers came in 1910: Rodney Horton and his wife of three years, Donna; Rodney's younger brother Arthur; his wife Mattie; their three-year-old daughter; and Mattie's mother Mary Saunders. The two men would leave the house during the day to sell jewelry and real estate in their respective jobs, but Mrs. Saunders plied her trade of dressmaker at home.[21]

Yet another bungalow book influenced the design of the Swiss-chalet-style bungalow built by the Wilson Company at 3008 Morrison (figs. 121 and 122).[22] The Los Angeles firm Ye Planry, which later moved to Dallas, published its first bungalow book in 1908, just as the first houses in Woodland Heights were being constructed. The bungalow at 3008 Morrison bears a striking resemblance to Ye Planry Design No. 328, except for the addition of the two dormer windows. The central porch, the shape of the porch pilasters, the pergola extending from only one side of the porch, the indented front entrance to a central living room, the placement of the front windows, and the decorative diamond patterns of the upper windows all are duplicated in the Woodland Heights bungalow. Described in the 1910 promotional brochure as "one of the finest specimens of the true bungalow type in Woodland Heights," this house was first owned by Hart Wartell, a barber, and his wife Katie.[23]

The designer who so assiduously studied these bungalow books and adapted their designs for the

Fig. 114. J. J. Bruce House, 3215 Morrison, Houston, built ca. 1908–1909. From Homes *2 (Feb., 1912): 6. Reproduction courtesy Houston Metropolitan Archives, Houston Public Library.*

Fig. 115. Design No. R-951, E. W. Stillwell, Representative California Homes, *p. 51.*

early Woodland Heights houses probably was a young man named Nelson McConnell Irvin. The Wilson Realty Company announced in 1908 that they had hired Irvin, then only eighteen years old, as "architect, designer, and decorator for these artistic and up-to-date homelike homes."[24] Irvin evidently learned his skills from his contractor father and from books. He was listed simply as a draftsman in the 1908 city directory, but in the 1910 directory his job with the Wilson Realty Company was reflected, and he listed himself as an architect. Later city directories show him working for the Wilson Realty Company through 1913. Irvin left Houston to serve in World War I and, when he returned, worked for the architectural and building firm of Russell Brown.[25]

Although many bungalow books were published in Los Angeles, the cradle of early bungalow de-

Fig. 116. 3302 Beauchamp, Houston, built ca. 1908–1909. From Woodland Heights, courtesy Travis Elementary School.

velopment, they also were produced in such varied places as Cedar Rapids, Iowa; Philadelphia, Pennsylvania; and Dallas, Texas. Ye Planry, the Dallas bungalow book firm, originated in Los Angeles, where it published the 1908 catalogue, *Ye Planry Bungalows,* which was used in Houston's Woodland Heights. The firm produced at least four more editions of its bungalow book in Los Angeles before it moved to Dallas in 1913. Owned and managed in Dallas by the brothers Floyd and L. T. Dernier, Ye Planry exhibited at the 1913 State Fair and published *Beautiful Homes* in 1914, the "first actual production of a bungalow book made in Texas."[26] The introduction to the book aptly de-

Fig. 117. Design No. 352, Henry L. Wilson, The Bungalow Book, p. 62.

Fig. 118. Design No. 394, Henry L. Wilson, The Bungalow Book, *p. 86.*

Fig. 119. Ward House, 3301 Morrison, Houston, built ca. 1908–1909. From Homes *2 (Mar., 1912): 6. Reproduction courtesy Houston Metropolitan Archives, Houston Public Library.*

scribed the eclectic collection of styles represented: "California bungalows, Swiss Chalets, Italian Villas, Spanish Haciendo [*sic*], Old English, French Chateau, Sullivanesque, and Frank Lloyd Wright types of homes."[27] A standard set of working plans and specifications ordered from the catalogue cost the customer ten dollars.

The Dernier brothers made a special effort to market Ye Planry's designs through retail lumber yards, supplying lumber yards across the state with their complete plan service, including books of photos, advertising copy, and detailed plans and specifications. Ye Planry also may have supplied the house plans sold through *Holland's Magazine.* Although there is no mention of Ye Planry in the Holland's articles, the authors of all the articles offering plans for sale were either employees or

Fig. 120. Rodney Horton House, 3301 Houston Ave., Houston, built ca. 1908–1909. From Woodland Heights, courtesy Travis Elementary School.

officers of Ye Planry. The bungalow at 305 Oldham in Waxahachie reinforces the link between *Holland's* and Ye Planry. It is a documented example of a house built according to plans from Ye Planry that bears a strong resemblance to a design published a few years later in *Holland's Magazine* (figs. 123 and 124).[28]

Other documented examples of Ye Planry houses have been found in Texas, but probably they were selected from the lumber yard service, for they do not match any of the designs in the 1914 catalogue *Beautiful Homes*. In Corsicana, the Ritters-

bacher House at 702 North 25th Street and the Westbrook House at 2201 West 4th Avenue both are documented as Ye Planry designs in the builder's contracts but do not match any of the plans in *Beautiful Homes*. The Texas General Contractors Association's *Monthly Bulletin* in the mid-1920s listed Ye Planry as the architect for houses to be built all over the state, but by that time their bungalow designs were being supplanted by other styles.[29]

Bungalow books continued to appear into the 1920s, and the term "bungalow" continued to be

Fig. 121. Wartell House, 3008 Morrison, Houston, built ca. 1908–1909. From Woodland Heights, courtesy Travis Elementary School.

Fig. 122. Design No. 328, Ye Planry Bungalows, *p. 52.*

Fig. 123. Jarrett House, 305 Oldham, Waxahachie, built 1916. Photo by the author.

used to describe small houses, even if they lacked the bungalow hallmarks of horizontal proportions and wide porches. George Palmer Telling, of Pasadena, California, was one of the publishers of these later bungalow books. He included "Spanish" and "Italian" bungalows among his designs, one of which, No. 901, probably influenced the Hicks House in Fort Worth (2400 Harrison Avenue; see figs. 125 and 126).[30] The porte-cochere was added and the roof lines altered to match other Telling designs, but the distinctive high central block; the lower, projecting front blocks; and the window pattern of the central block all duplicate Telling's Design No. 90. The first owner of the house was Harry Hicks, president of the King Midas Oil and Gas Association, Ltd.

The Bungalowcraft Company of Los Angeles

Fig. 124. Design No. 2497, in Holland's Magazine *(June, 1920): 22. Reproduction courtesy Houston Public Library.*

Fig. 125. *Design No. 901, George P. Telling,* Telling Plan Book: Spanish and Italian Bungalows.

published *Homes of the Moment* in 1929, at the end of the bungalow era, just before the Depression drastically curtailed homebuilding. The authors described it as "a book on bungalow building in its latest development," and they included an excerpt from a letter by another Texan, Carl F. Hammer of El Paso: "Have received plans and they sure have met with my approval, it truly is a 'home, not a house.'"[31]

Fig. 126. *Hicks House, 2400 Harrison Ave., Fort Worth, built ca. 1920.* Photo by the author.

6

· · · · ·

Ready-Made Residences

READY-CUT HOUSE CATALOGUES

We have now completed our new home,
built from your Modern Home Plan No. 119. We could
not have been better suited by employing a first class
architect at many times the cost.

—C. H. Carl, Hereford, Texas

C. H. Carl wrote these words to Sears, Roebuck and Company after ordering and building a two-story frame house in Hereford from a Sears catalogue (fig. 127).[1] Sears house catalogues probably are the most widely known of the ready-cut, or pre-cut, variety, which sold the building materials for a house in pre-cut form along with the plans needed to assemble the pieces. However, Sears had plenty of competitors in the ready-cut house catalogue business, including two firms based in Houston.

Ready-cut houses were not uncommon in pre–Civil War Texas, although other terms, such as "ready-made," were used to describe them. Given the shortage of locally produced building materials and of skilled craftsmen, houses and other buildings often were prepared in the Northeast and shipped in pieces to Texas. However, most of these houses probably never appeared in catalogues but were sent in response to specific orders or even sent on speculation to a market that couldn't afford to be choosy about the style or appearance of the buildings bought. The *Civilian and Galveston Gazette* of January 18, 1840, carried a notice that the "lumber for a Ware House 64 x 100 feet, with shingles" was for sale. Such ready-cut buildings also found a market in the years immediately after the Civil War, before local industries were able to recover or develop following the war's disruption. In 1866, the Bangor, Maine, firm of Fogg and Pattoe sent ten ready-made houses by ship to Galveston, along with craftsmen to assemble them. Thomas R. Bolling, a Galveston grocer, purchased one of these houses, according to a newspaper account.[2]

After the Civil War, catalogues of ready-cut houses began to appear, featuring, for the most part, small houses intended for frontier situations or for use as summer cabins. Some of these smaller

MODERN HOME No. 119

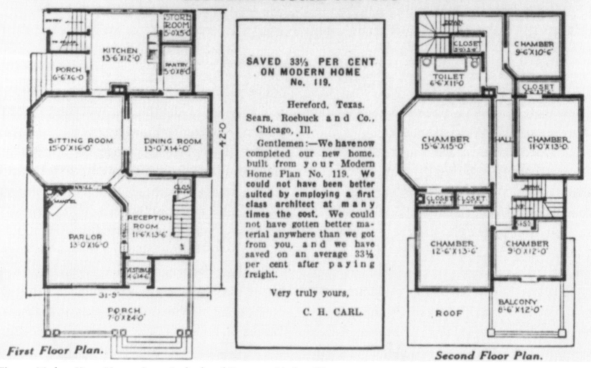

SAVED 33⅓ PER CENT
ON MODERN HOME
No. 119.

Hereford, Texas.
Sears, Roebuck and Co.,
Chicago, Ill.

Gentlemen:—We have now
completed our new home,
built from your Modern
Home Plan No. 119. We
could not have been better
suited by employing a first
class architect at many
times the cost. We could
not have gotten better material anywhere than we got
from you, and we have
saved on an average 33½
per cent after paying
freight.

Very truly yours,

C. H. CARL.

First Floor Plan.

Second Floor Plan.

Fig. 127. Modern Home No. 119, Sears, Roebuck and Company, Modern Homes, *p. 93.*

structures were shipped as prefabricated panels, or sections, to be assembled, rather than as completely unassembled pieces. The early Sears house catalogues, beginning with the 1908 *Book of Modern Homes and Building Plans*, changed this pattern by marketing substantial one- and two-story houses intended for year-round use.[3] The designs were not complex or highly decorated, but were intended to represent "modern" designs and to utilize the quality materials for which Sears was known. C. H. Carl's house in Hereford, built around 1910, was a relatively simple, "modern" Sears design, with no money wasted on exterior decorative flourishes (fig. 127). However, it was more complex than a basic foursquare house, for it had front and side gables projecting from the main hipped roof, a second-floor balcony above the entrance porch, and bay windows for the sitting room and one of the bedrooms. The substantial size of the house, with five upstairs bedrooms, suited the Carls, who intended to use it as a boarding house.[4]

Sears soon became more style-conscious in its house catalogues. The simple, no-frills designs never disappeared from the catalogues, but they were joined by others in a wide variety of popular styles. J. T. Marnson selected one of the early Sears bungalows, Modern Home No. 264P234 (fig. 128), for construction in Ladonia and was pleased enough with the results to write: "Being the first house built of materials ordered of you in this neighborhood, it was visited by many spectators and pronounced by all superior to any they had ever seen. My carpenter has followed the trade for 18 years and said the material was the best he had ever used."[5]

The Carl House and the Marnson House have not survived, but other houses matching Sears designs can be found across Texas. The house built in Houston (747 E. 6½ Street) in 1922 for contractor John W. King and his wife Willie reproduced another bungalow design that appeared in multiple Sears catalogues (figs. 129 and 130).[6]

Several companies entered the ready-cut house

Fig. 128. Modern Home No. 264P234, Sears, Roebuck and Company, Modern Homes, *p. 10.*

Fig. 129. J. W. King House, 747 E. 6½ St., Houston, built ca. 1924. Photo by the author.

Fig. 130. Modern Home No. 264P244, Sears Roebuck and Company, Modern Homes, *p. 33.*

catalogue business around the same time as Sears and continued to provide stiff competition through the years, particularly the Gordon–Van Tine Company, in Davenport, Iowa; and the Aladdin Company, in Bay City, Michigan. Ernest F. Hodgson's Massachusetts firm began offering panelized vacation cottages in 1902, added year-round homes several years later, and continued to produce house catalogues until the 1970s, long after the Sears ready-cut division and its other competitors had gone out of business.

Ready-cut houses were ideal for companies wanting to build workers' housing quickly and cheaply. Sears featured photographs of streets of company-built Sears houses in several of their catalogues, and the Aladdin Company even published a special catalogue for companies interested in such

Fig. 131. *Crain Ready-Cut houses built for the Texas Company at Parks Camp, near Breckenridge. From Crain Ready-Cut House Company,* Ready-Cut and Sectional Houses, Catalogue No. 5, *pp. 32–33.* Reproduction courtesy Houston Metropolitan Research Center, Houston Public Library.

construction. That catalogue, *Aladdin Plan of Industrial Housing,* offered to supply "anything from a single house, with its complete heating, lighting and plumbing equipment, to a complete city—sewers, walks, pavements, lighting and water works systems, stores, schools, churches, hotels and dwelling houses."[7] Although the catalogue indicated that Aladdin industrial housing had been built in Texas, it did not identify the location or the purchasing company.

Such Aladdin housing could well have been bought by an oil company, for, in the early years of the twentieth century, Texas's booming oil industry needed workers' housing constructed quickly near the many new drilling sites that were in sparsely populated areas. In 1919, the Gulf Pipe Line Company purchased ready-cut workers' houses from the Crain Ready-Cut House Company of Houston, for assembly in Big Sandy, Breckenridge, Burkburnett, Fort Worth, Garland, and Greenville.[8] Crain also supplied ready-cut houses to the Texas Company for Parks Camp, near Breckenridge, and illustrated them in one of its catalogues (fig. 131).[9]

The Crain Ready-Cut House Company and the T. J. Williams Manufacturing Company, both based in Houston, appear to have been the major Texas producers of ready-cut houses and catalogues, al-

though for a single year, a Woodward and Hardie, Inc., advertised itself as a manufacturer of ready-cut houses in the 1926 San Antonio city directory.[10]

T. J. Williams established his company first, in 1915, and published the catalogue *Better Built Homes for Less Money* the same year (fig. 132). Williams had been in the lumber industry for several years and had owned a sawmill in Honey Island

Fig. 132. *Design on cover of T. J. Williams,* Better Built Homes for Less Money. Reproduction courtesy Gene Crain, Houston.

Fig. 133. *Advertisement for the T. J. Williams House Manufacturing Company, in* Gulf Coast Lumberman *3 (Nov. 15, 1915): 18. Reproduction courtesy Special Collections and Archives, University of Houston Libraries.*

ber and Manufacturing Company, and that name later was changed to the Crain Ready-Cut House Company. The new catalogues dropped any mention of the single thick wall construction and displayed a far greater variety of house designs. Crain published catalogues for both permanent and portable ready-cut houses, with the designs for the permanent houses in a wide range of styles (fig. 134). Many were particularly well suited to the Gulf Coast climate and featured prominent screened porches, a rarity in other catalogues of the period.[14]

The Crain Ready-Cut House Company survived into the 1940s and was said to have constructed ten thousand homes and other buildings by 1940.[15] E. L. Crain and his Ready-Cut House Company were

before developing his "single thick wall" construction technique for ready-cut houses, using primarily boards measuring two by six inches, with no studding. His catalogue described the houses as being 50 percent stronger than traditional construction and "absolutely dust, bug, vermin and rat proof."[11] Being familiar with the lumber industry, Williams realized how threatened retail lumber dealers felt by ready-cut house companies that could circumvent dealers and sell directly to the consumer. Williams consequently tried to work with local dealers and use them as agents.[12]

Most of the Williams houses were very basic bungalows with hipped roofs and small, triangular front gables above the front porches (fig. 133). The most elaborate was a two-story Prairie-Style model called the "Montrose" after the successful Houston neighborhood laid out in 1911. Williams bungalows were built in Houston, Port Arthur, and San Antonio, but the "single thick wall" never revolutionized house construction, and only two years after Williams started the company, he sold it to Houston real estate dealer and developer Edward Lillo Crain.[13]

The company was renamed the E. L. Crain Lum-

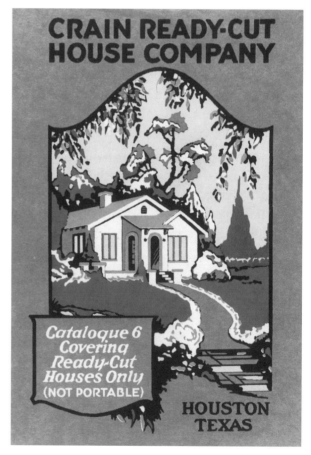

Fig. 134. *Catalogue cover from Crain Ready-Cut House Company,* Crain Ready-Cut House Company, Catalogue 6. Reproduction courtesy Gene Crain, Houston.

Fig. 135. 1608 Haver St., Houston, built 1922. Photo by the author.

involved in the development of several Houston subdivisions, including Cherryhurst, Brady Home, Garden Oaks, Pineview Place, and Southside Place. The house at 1608 Haver Street, matching Design No. M-213, was built in 1922 in the Cherryhurst subdivision of Houston by Crain's company. Crain sold the house that same year to W. N. Finnegan, Jr., who worked in the offices of the Humble Oil and Refining Company (figs. 135 and 136).[16]

Owners and managers of retail lumber yards felt threatened by ready-cut house catalogues, viewing local orders of ready-cut houses as lost sales. T .J. Williams's short-lived effort to sell ready-cut houses through retail lumber yards evidently was not emulated by other ready-cut house manufacturers. Retail lumber trade publications, including the *Gulf Coast Lumberman,* published in Houston, featured numerous articles about the mail-order

Fig. 136. Plan No. M-213, Crain Ready-Cut House Company, Ready-Cut Homes, Catalogue No. 4.

Fig. 137. Illustration for the article "A Dealer Without Plans Is Like a Tailor Without Patterns," Gulf Coast Lumberman 5 (June 15, 1917): 6. Reproduction courtesy Special Collections and Archives, University of Houston Libraries.

threat, bearing titles such as "Fighting Ready-Cut Houses" and "Readi-Cut-Itis."[17] Advertising and the use of plan books, or house catalogues, were presented as the best methods by which retail lumber yards could fight the ready-cut threat.

Displaying catalogues of house plans for the use of customers became a common practice in retail lumber yards, partly in response to the ready-cut threat and partly in conjunction with general campaigns to encourage home building and the corresponding lumber sales. A particularly charming illustration used by the *Gulf Coast Lumberman* in this context shows, in silhouette, a retail lumber dealer presenting a house catalogue to an eager couple with the caption, "A dealer without plans is like a tailor without patterns" (fig. 137).[18] The Dallas firm of Ye Planry marketed their catalogues to retail lumber yards as part of this movement, presenting their service as the answer to questions about how to meet mail-order competition and increase sales.[19] In 1915, William Cameron and Company contracted with Ye Planry to install their plan-book system in thirty-five Cameron lumber yards in Texas and other parts of the Southwest.[20] The Hillyer-Deutsch-Jarratt lumber yard in San Antonio adopted the Porter-Ballard plan books and started advertising heavily in the local news-

papers. One of their ads won first place in the 1915 Lumberman's Association of Texas advertising contest (fig. 138).[21]

Widespread national advertising by the successful ready-cut firms, local advertising and promotions by threatened retail lumber yards, and continually multiplying catalogues of plans and houses bombarded consumers with images of idyllic homes and promises of a resultant transformation in the quality of their lives. This media promotion may have generated unreasonable expectations on the part of a few consumers, but the scale of its distribution inevitably increased public awareness of house styles and designs to a level far beyond what had been possible in the past.

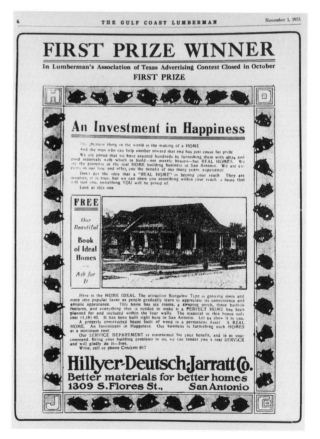

Fig. 138. Winning advertisement by the Hillyer-Deutsch-Jarratt Company of San Antonio, printed in Gulf Coast Lumberman 3 (Nov. 1, 1915): 6. Reproduction courtesy Special Collections and Archives, University of Houston Libraries.

7

. . . . .

Context of a Community

WAXAHACHIE HOUSES BASED ON PUBLISHED DESIGNS

Waxahachie . . . is substantially built, the business portion
consisting of modern two and three story brick and
stone buildings, and the residence portion of neat and
elegant homes, many of them being very costly. It is perhaps
the best built city of its size in the state.

—*J. T. Cole, in W. W. Dexter,* Texas: Imperial State of America
with Her Diadem of Cities, *1904*

Although the author of these words was a town promoter and undoubtedly prejudiced in its favor, Waxahachie today still contains a "residence portion of neat and elegant homes,"[1] many of them dating from the town's heyday in the late nineteenth and early twentieth centuries. Several of these remaining houses, along with others that have not survived, can be attributed to designs in published sources, and by looking at them within the context of the community that produced them, we can gain a better understanding of the use of published designs in Texas during this period.

Located thirty miles south of Dallas, Waxahachie served as the seat of Ellis County from its establishment in 1850. The town grew slowly until after the Civil War, when agricultural and commercial activity began to increase. A small Methodist college, Marvin College, was established in 1870, and the county's first stone courthouse re-

placed a wooden one in 1874. When rail service finally reached the town in 1879, economic activity surged even more, particularly in the cotton industry, and the population grew accordingly. Waxahachie's 1870 population of 1,354 more than doubled to 3,076 in 1890 and doubled again in the next twenty years, reaching 6,205 in 1910. New houses were needed to shelter the newcomers, and extra-special houses were needed for those residents who managed to benefit most from the economic activity of the town. Those special houses often were based upon designs published in catalogues and magazines.

At least seven Waxahachie houses built between 1891 and 1900 were based on published designs: the Dunlap House (1891), based on a design from *Shoppell's Modern Houses;* the Patrick House (1899–1900), based on a design published in the magazine *Scientific American Architect's and Builders Edition;*

Fig. 139. "Bird's-eye View of Waxahachie." Fold-out postcard, ca. 1904.

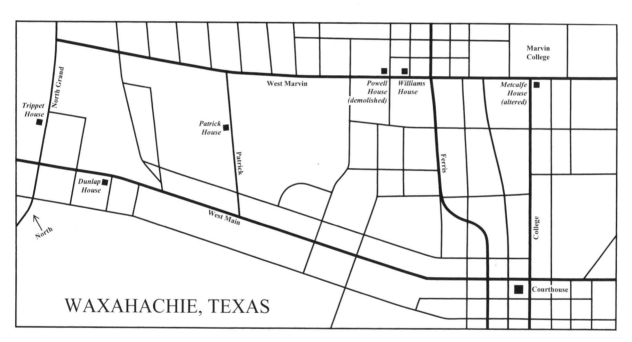

Map by Neal vonHedemann

and five houses based on George F. Barber designs, the Powell House (1892), the Williams House (1893), the Hosford House (circa 1895), the Metcalfe House (1894), and the Trippet House (1895).

The owners of these houses all were prosperous members of Waxahachie's upper-middle class. However, most of them had started with few ad-

vantages and had worked hard to establish themselves and their families in the young, growing community. The new houses served to demonstrate their owners' positions and success, while also improving the appearance and reputation of the town. The use of designs from published sources would have helped to insure that visitors

and residents would recognize the houses as tasteful, up-to-date, and fitting homes for prominent members of the community. No records survive to tell us how the design decisions were made and what these owners thought of their houses, but research into the lives and careers of the owners does provide some clues.

The earliest of these houses (1203 W. Main Street) was built in 1890–91 for Oscar E. Dunlap, who had been elected president of the Waxahachie Citizen's Bank four years earlier and who continued in that position until the year of his death in 1925 (figs. 140 and 141). Referred to as "Judge" in deference to his four years as a county judge between 1882 and 1886, Dunlap's rise to prominence had not been easy. His father had been a successful wholesale grocer and cotton farmer in Mississippi, but the Civil War ruined him financially. The family moved to Texas in 1867, when Oscar was eighteen years old. They settled in Ellis County a year later, where Oscar helped with the family farm for almost ten years, until he married the stepdaughter of a successful farmer and landowner and was elected justice of the peace. He studied law while serving in this office and was admitted to the bar in 1880. His rise after that was rapid, with elec-

tion to the office of county judge in 1882 and 1884. He ceased practicing law when he was elected president of Citizen's Bank in 1886, and thereafter he concentrated his energies on the bank and other business and community interests, including the street railroad and the electric company. Eventually he served as president of the Texas State Bankers Association and on the executive council of the American Bankers Association.[2]

Dunlap built his new house at the age of forty, evidently feeling secure enough after four years as county judge and four successful years at the bank to invest in a house large enough to be valued on the tax rolls at three thousand dollars. His previous house had been valued at half that amount. At the time the new house was built, Dunlap had been married to his wife Ella for fourteen years, and they had two children, Estelle, aged twelve years, and Oscar, aged six years. We do not know who the builder was, or whether Ella was involved in the selection of the design for the house. However, either Dunlap, Ella, or their builder must have had access to issues of the magazine *Shoppell's Modern Houses* or one of Shoppell's house catalogues, for the Dunlap House clearly reproduces Shoppell's Design No. 438.[3]

Fig. 140. O. E. Dunlap House, 1203 W. Main St., Waxahachie, built 1890–91. Photo by the author.

Fig. 141. Design No. 438, in Shoppell's Modern Houses 2 (Jan., 1887): 18.

The house is a pleasing composition of Queen Anne stylistic elements, including an asymmetrical façade, corner tower, patterned shingle siding, and decorative woodwork on the porches, eaves, and gables. The changes from the original design were minimal. The plan was reversed, shifting the tower to the opposite side of the façade to take advantage of the orientation of the corner site, and the projecting bay on the other side of the façade was increased in size. The small central dormer window, included in the Shoppell design but missing from the house today, originally was part of the structure, as an early photograph of the house shows (fig. 142). Although it is an imposing residence, set on ground slightly higher than the street, it is not overwhelming in size.

Dunlap selected the site for his house in the new

Fig. 142. O. E. Dunlap House, 1203 W. Main St., Waxahachie, soon after construction completed, ca. 1891. Courtesy Ellis County Museum, Waxahachie.

West End Addition of Waxahachie, which had been laid out the year before and was being developed in a manner consistent with the ideas of the garden suburb movement of the late nineteenth century. The lots were large, and the developers built a park-like ellipse at the far end of the development. A mule-drawn streetcar carried residents the one mile from the ellipse to the courthouse square and business district. Dunlap was among the first to build in the new development, but he was followed by many prosperous businessmen, including at least two others who built houses based on published designs, H. W. Trippet and M. T. Patrick.

The Dunlaps lived in the house for thirty years before a series of misfortunes began to strike the family at four-year intervals. In 1921, their son, Oscar Jr., at the age of thirty-seven, was killed in a collision with an interurban train on Christmas Eve, as he was driving from his home in Dallas to visit the family in Waxahachie. Oscar Jr.'s death was a severe blow to his father, and four years later the Judge died of pneumonia, following what the newspaper described as a nervous breakdown. Daughter Estelle, who never had married and who continued to live at home, died only four years after that, at the age of fifty-one. Her mother lived on in the house for four more years, until her death in 1933. The funeral services for all four were held in the turreted house on Main Street, which, although no longer fashionable, was firmly identified with this influential family by the members of the community.

In 1892, a year after Oscar Dunlap completed his house based on a Shoppell design, a Waxahachie lawyer, Fines P. Powell, built a house based on a

Fig. 143. Ed Williams House, 412 W. Marvin St., Waxahachie. Photo by the author.

George F. Barber catalogue design (fig. 58).[4] The thirty-eight-year-old Powell and his eighteen-year-old wife Myrtle had been married for only three months when they contracted with builder W. H. Smith to construct what was described in the mechanic's lien as a "two-story dwelling house consisting of four rooms on the lower floor and three rooms on the upper floor" for the sum of three thousand dollars.[5] The house no longer survives, but a photograph remains to document its resemblance to Barber's Design No. 56, published in his *Cottage Souvenir No. 2* (1891) and again in his *Cottage Souvenir, Revised and Enlarged* (1892) (fig. 57). Powell built the house about a half-mile north of the town square on a lot down the street from the former Marvin College building, which had been taken over by the city for a public school.

Barber's highly decorative Design No. 56, with its Moorish gingerbread arches on the second-floor gallery and its polygonal cupola interrupting the front gable, appealed to other Texans in addition to Powell, as we saw in chapter 3. Barber gave two possible floor plans for the design in his catalogue *Cottage Souvenir No. 2,* a larger one with an estimated cost of $3,900; and a smaller one, lacking the dressing rooms, servant's room, and rear balcony on the second floor, with a cost of only $2,900. Powell evidently chose the smaller of the two plans, for his loan from the savings association was for $3,000, and the house was described in the mechanic's lien as having only three rooms on the upper floor, as Barber's smaller plan did.

We do not know who selected the design of the Powell House, but certainly it is conceivable that the young bride Myrtle was involved. As a schoolteacher before her marriage, first president of the Waxahachie Shakespeare Club, and the daughter of a newspaper editor, she was educated and undoubtedly was familiar with popular magazines. She easily could have seen one of Barber's advertisements in the *Ladies' Home Journal* or another magazine and ordered a catalogue. Powell himself had been satisfied with a house valued at $1,000 on the tax rolls until he married Myrtle and borrowed the $3,000 necessary for the new house. His law practice, combined with investments in land, evidently were sufficient to support the house, for he paid off his loan early, after only four years. Two children soon were born to fill the extra rooms on the second floor.[6]

Grocery-store owner Ed Williams or his wife Ella evidently liked the design of the Powells' house, for they built a variation on it just across the street (412 W. Marvin) within the next year (fig. 143). Ed and Ella, too, were newlyweds when they built the house, although Ella was a widow with a twelve-year-old son when she married thirty-year-old Ed in 1893. Ed's father, John G. Williams, was a successful banker and businessman and an early resident of Waxahachie, who had served as mayor from 1874 to 1876 and was a member of the city council when he died, only a month before Ed married Ella. According to his obituary, Ed's father was well-known for his honor, public responsibility, and success in business. Ed's new house, which was started soon after the wedding, undoubtedly was

Fig. 144. Hosford House, 3209 Highway 77N, near Waxahachie, built ca. 1894–95, significantly altered in later years. Photo ca. 1900. Courtesy Ellis County Museum, Waxahachie.

a symbol of his new independence from his father, as well as his change in marital status.[7]

Although John G. Williams left his estate to his widow, Cynisca, he gave substantial gifts to his children not long before his death, including $5,000 to Ed.[8] It was probably that gift that enabled Ed to build his new house, which cost over $6,400. He started paying for the construction of his new house in cash, but evidently the cash ran out before the house was completed, and he was compelled to give mechanic's liens on the house for the amounts still owing to the lumber yards and to his builder, C. J. Griggs.[9]

Any number of factors could explain Ed's financial difficulties, and no definitive documentary proof exists. He might have lost part of the money intended for his new house through gambling, for the name Ed Williams appears three times in county records with gaming charges between 1892 and 1894. However, there were three taxpayers in the county with that name in 1893, and our house-building Ed Williams could have lost his money in thoroughly legal ways. He was able to complete the payments to builder and lumber yards in 1895 and cleared the liens on the house. Unfortunately, by 1898 he shows up in the civil court records being prosecuted for bad debts. In the 1900 census, he gave his occupation as farmer, rather than merchant; and in 1902 he sold the house he had built for his bride. Although surviving documents do not solve the mystery of whether Ed was unlucky in business or gambling, it is interesting to note that his mother, in her will, left Ed's share of her estate to his son, rather than to Ed.[10]

Since the Ed Williams House was built across the street from the Powell House, it appropriately enough was not an exact copy of Barber's Design No. 56, but it clearly was based on that design. There are no records to indicate whether Williams wrote to Barber for a custom design or had the builder, C. J. Griggs, adapt the design of the Powell House. Whoever actually adapted the design dispensed

with the central tower interrupting the front gable but kept the projecting two-story front porch, as well as the dormer window in the hipped roof and the bay-windowed, front-gabled section projecting forward on one side of the house. The tiny triangular balcony on the outside corner of the second-floor bay also was retained. The elaborate gingerbread millwork decorating the porches is different from that used in the Powell House, particularly the distinctive horseshoe-shaped element in the lower half of the projecting porch, which resembles one used in Barber's Design No. 53, also from *Cottage Souvenir No. 2.* The mechanic's lien for the house indicates that the decorative millwork for the house was ordered from a Dallas merchant, rather than from the local Waxahachie lumber yard that supplied the rest of the building materials.

The design of the Ed Williams House was duplicated exactly when William Hosford built a new house on his property in the country north of town (3209 Highway 77N; fig. 144). No records survive regarding the construction, but a descendent of Hosford dates the house to ca. 1894–95 and indicates that, according to family tradition, the same builder was used for both houses.[11]

The same Barber-designed Powell House that inspired the Williams and the Hosford Houses probably impressed yet another Waxahachie resident. Banker John J. Metcalfe did not copy the Powell House design, but he did use the same mail-order architect, George F. Barber. As secretary of the Ellis County Building and Savings Association, from which Powell had obtained financing for his house, Metcalfe would have examined the house plans, as well as Powell's financial situation, before signing the loan papers. Metcalfe must have liked what he saw, for, even though he undoubtedly looked at a variety of house plans in his position at the Ellis County Building and Savings Association, when he and his wife Ella decided to build a new house, they ordered plans from Barber. Their 1894 contract with the builder D. A. Cook specifi-

Fig. 145. J. J. Metcalfe House, 520 N. College, Waxahachie, built 1894, significantly altered in later years. Photo ca. 1900. Courtesy Ellis County Museum, Waxahachie.

cally states that the plans and specifications were made by George F. Barber.[12]

Unlike the Powells and the Williamses, John and Ella Metcalfe were not newlyweds when they decided to build a new house. Both were in their forties, and they had been married for over twenty years and had four children. Like the Dunlap House, the Metcalfes' house signified financial success and stability, finally obtained in mid-life, rather than a change in marital status. John Metcalfe was born in Kentucky and lived in Ohio and Indiana before coming to Texas sometime before 1880. He appears in the 1880 census, living with his brother-in-law in the country near Waxahachie, but no occupation is given for him. However, by 1890,

Fig. 146. Design No. 84, George F. Barber, New Model Dwellings. *Reproduction courtesy of the Frances Loeb Library, Graduate School of Design, Harvard University.*

Fig. 147. H. W. Trippet House, 209 N. Grand Ave., Waxahachie, built 1895. Photo ca. 1904, from W. W. Dexter, Texas Imperial State of America. *Reproduction courtesy University of Houston Libraries.*

when the Waxahachie National Bank was established, Metcalfe had made enough money to be one of the stockholders, in addition to holding the position of assistant cashier. He moved up to the position of cashier in 1891, before taking the position of secretary of the Ellis County Building and Savings Association sometime before 1894, when he signed Powell's loan. He remained on the board of directors of the Waxahachie National Bank for several years after he left the position of cashier.[13]

John had his and Ella's house built on a large corner lot (520 N. College) across the street from the old Marvin College building, several blocks north of the courthouse square. The exterior of the house has been drastically altered, but a photo-

graph survives showing the original Queen Anne design that matches a design published in Barber's catalogue *New Model Dwellings* (figs. 145 and 146).[14] The catalogue first was published in 1894, the year that the Metcalfes contracted with D. A. Cook to build their house.

After the house was completed, Metcalfe was pleased enough to write the following testimonial letter, which Barber included in an 1899 booklet: "Concerning my house, the selection of which was made from your catalogue, I beg to say that I am well pleased with my home from your plans as they are perfect and complete in every particular, so when the builder takes hold of them, they 'fit in' like a 'puzzle.' The most satisfactory part about your plans is, your house needs no extras when completed. I heartily recommend your plans for modern homes."[15]

H. W. Trippet probably ordered a custom design from Barber when he decided to build a new house for his family in 1896 (209 N. Grand Avenue; see fig. 147). We know from the mechanic's lien that Barber was the architect; and, since the house does not match any of the designs in Barber's catalogues exactly, the design likely was the result of a special order.[16] Trippet could well have gotten the idea from Metcalfe, since both men were associated with the Waxahachie National Bank from its beginning. Trippet served as cashier when the bank was organized, and in 1891, when Metcalfe became cashier, Trippet was elected president of the bank.[17] However, the design that Trippet ordered from Barber was very different from the Metcalfes', even though the essential elements described in the two mechanic's liens were quite similar: both were two-story frame houses with shingle roofs and brick chimneys, and each cost five thousand dollars to build. Trippet's house had ten rooms, as opposed to Metcalfe's nine, but that mention of one extra room does little to indicate how much larger and more imposing the Trippet House would have appeared, compared with the Metcalfe House.

Trippet's house evidently was meant to be imposing and to serve as a symbol of his success, and it remains one of the most impressive of Waxahachie's surviving nineteenth-century houses. Undoubtedly it was among the largest houses in town, in terms of square-footage and height when it was built; and its design elements and siting all add to the impression of height and mass, making it seem even larger than it is. Trippet selected a large, three-acre plot of land in the West End Addition, with few other houses in the immediate neighborhood. One of the house's most noticeable features is the corner tower that emerges from the roof at the attic level and has an unusually tall, elongated, bulbous roof with a decorative finial that stretches its height

even further. The mass of the house is emphasized by the two-story gallery that curves around two sides of the house. Unlike the smaller galleries of the Metcalfe House, the Trippet House galleries, encompassed by the main hipped roof, appear to extend the body of the house outward.

The simple, slender, rounded columns are in the Colonial Revival style, which still was in an early phase of its popularity at the time. Barber's design for the house represents a transition from Queen Anne to Colonial Revival. The basic form of the house, with its asymmetrical façade, corner tower, and steeply pitched roof, echoes the familiar Queen Anne style houses that had been built by numerous successful Texas businessmen, including Judge Dunlap. The Colonial Revival decorative elements would have added the distinction of a new style to the structure's already-impressive size.

Hosea W. Trippet was the second of ten children born to Aaron and Martha Trippet. The family moved from Missouri to Texas in 1861, when Hosea was eight, and farmed until after the Civil War, when Aaron started a dry goods and grocery business. For years, Trippet worked with his father and lived at home, until, at the age of twenty-eight, he married Mamie Amsley in 1881. His father helped to organize the Waxahachie National Bank in 1890 and served as its first president, while Trippet worked as cashier. His election to the bank's presidency the next year signaled a definite improvement in his status. The local paper announced that Trippet had bought S. W. King's "handsome residence on Main Street" only a few months after he took over at the bank. A few years later, in January 1895, Trippet purchased all the stock of his father's store and took over its management. Evidently he felt a need for a new and larger house, in accord with his new position within the community. In June 1895, he purchased the lot in the West End Addition; and in November 1895, he signed a contract commissioning C. J. Griggs to build a ten-room frame house according to plans by George F. Barber of Knoxville, Tennessee.[18]

Fig. 148. M. T. Patrick House, 233 Patrick St., Waxahachie, built 1899–1900. Photo taken a few years after construction completed. Courtesy Emily K. Graham, Waxahachie.

Fig. 149. House design by Joseph W. Northrup of Bridgeport, Conn., in Scientific American, Architects and Builders Edition 13 *(May, 1892): 67.*

CAPT. MARSHALL T. PATRICK

Fig. 150. Marshall T. Patrick. Courtesy Emily K. Graham, Waxahachie.

Unfortunately Trippet may have overextended himself financially in building the house, or perhaps competition in the dry goods business cut into his expected profits. Whatever the cause of his financial difficulties, when he was faced with them, Trippet chose to keep his grand new house rather than selling it to support his business. In 1897, only a year after the house was completed, Trippet sold the dry goods store back to his father. His assessed tax valuation for that year totaled only $5,645, of which $5,000 represented the value of the house. This figure stands in stark contrast to his 1895 assessment of $26,745. During the next few years, Trippet struggled to hang onto his house and his reputation, and the local newspaper continued to mention him and his family in its version of a so-

ciety column: Mr. and Mrs. Trippet hosted a "lawn fete" for their church group, daughter Annie Laurie entertained her cousin from Fort Worth, and Trippet made a couple of trips to Joplin, Missouri.[19] No reasons were given in the paper for the trips to Missouri, but one can conjecture that they may have been part of an effort by Trippet to reestablish himself financially. Evidently nothing worked out. H. W. Trippet finally sold the house in 1900 and moved his wife and five children to a rented house in Fort Worth that same year. In the 1910 census, he appears in Mangum, Oklahoma, working as a grocer and still living with his family in rented housing.[20]

Marshall T. Patrick, president of the First National Bank of Waxahachie, had far better luck with his career, and his descendants still live in the house

Fig. 151. Emma Patrick. Courtesy Emily K. Graham, Waxahachie.

he had built based on a design published in *The Scientific American, Architects and Builders Edition* (233 Patrick Street; figs. 148 and 149). Patrick was more firmly established and older than Trippet and Dunlap when he built this house, giving his age as fifty-eight in the 1900 census, the year the house was completed (fig. 150). Born in Tennessee, Patrick moved to Waxahachie after the Civil War. He operated a freighting business and then a grocery, before helping in 1881 to found the private bank that in 1883 became Waxahachie's First National Bank. He remained active in banking over the years but also invested heavily in land and livestock.[21]

Patrick, along with his wife and three daughters, had lived for many years in a house on Franklin Street, a couple of blocks away from the square. The entire family moved to Nashville for the daughters to attend finishing school, and Patrick made regular trips back to Waxahachie to check on his property and investments. In the late 1890s, the family moved back and rented a house in the West End Addition until their new house was built.[22]

The three daughters, all unmarried young ladies in their twenties at the time, could well have been involved in the design decisions for the new house that was to serve as the setting for their social activities. In support of the involvement of at least one of the daughters, family legend includes a story that the oldest daughter, Emma (fig. 151), had wanted a brick Colonial design until the builder, C. J. Griggs, convinced her that the land on the site would not properly support the weight of a large brick structure.[23]

The design that finally was agreed upon was the product of architect Joseph W. Northrup of Bridgeport, Connecticut, and had been published in the May 1892 issue of the *Scientific American, Architects and Builders Edition*. It was one of only two designs in the issue that were illustrated in color, as well as black and white. Emma did not get her brick Colonial house, but she did get Colonial details, including the slender, classical porch col-

Fig. 152. Annie Patrick. Courtesy Emily K. Graham, Waxahachie.

umns, the decoration in the gable above the porch entrance, and the Palladian window in the third-floor front gable. However, these Colonial elements, like those of the Trippet House, were attached to a basic Queen Anne form, with a prominent corner tower, asymmetrical façade, shingle siding, and steeply pitched roofs.

The house was set on a ten-acre plot of land in the western part of town, not far from the Trippet and Dunlap houses; and its size, style, and site would have communicated the wealth and importance of the Patrick family to any passerby at the turn of the twentieth century. It served its owners well as a symbol of their position in the community and as a setting for social events, weddings, and funerals. Daughter Annie (fig. 152) was married in the house three years after it was completed, and she and her husband then moved into a smaller house that was built for them next door. Funeral services for all five family members also were held in the house, including the one for daughter Emma, who never married and lived in the house until her death in 1969, at the age of ninety-four.

The owners of these houses were representative members of Waxahachie's upper-middle class. Some were longtime residents of the city; others were relative newcomers. Their occupations varied; bankers predominated, but merchants, lawyers, and a farmer were represented. Most were active in efforts to promote the development and improvement of the town, economically, politically, and culturally. Powell served on a welcoming committee when Governor Hogg visited Waxahachie in 1892, Patrick chaired the building committee of the Cumberland Presbyterian Church, Dunlap was a library trustee, Trippet was an officer of the local Odd-Fellows lodge, and Myrtle Powell was the first president of the Waxahachie Shakespeare Club. Their houses announced their places within the community, and when some of them had to sell their houses for financial reasons, as Trippet and Williams did, apparently they did so with great reluctance.

The craftsmen who built these houses were not nearly as prosperous as the owners and left fewer traces in documents and records. We do not even know who built two of the houses; but, through mechanic's liens, we know that C. J. Griggs built the Williams and Trippet houses, D. A. Cook built the Metcalfe House, and W. H. Smith built the Powell House. Patrick family records indicate that C. J. Griggs also built the Patrick House. All three of these builders were relative newcomers to Waxahachie, arriving sometime after the 1880 census to take advantage of the building boom that accompanied the town's economic growth in the 1880s and 1890s.

C. J. Griggs, the most firmly established of the three, did not become a professional builder until he was in his thirties. In 1880, when he was thirty-two years old and living in Limestone County, he told the census-taker that his occupation was farmer. Soon after, he must have left farming for full-time work as a carpenter-builder, for, by 1886, he and his family had settled in Waxahachie. By 1892 the total value of his taxable property was a respectable $2,921, of which $2,500 was the value of his house. (In comparison, F. P. Powell's total that same year was $4,295, and John Metcalfe's was $4,540.) Griggs built modest cottages as well as the grand Trippet House, and he lived in the same neighborhood where he constructed the Williams House. His eldest daughter became a schoolteacher in Waxahachie, and his son a salesman.[24]

Published designs followed many paths in reaching the hands of builders such as C. J. Griggs. The builder himself could order catalogues and magazines and copy or adapt the designs pictured within to fit the requirements of clients requesting designs. Potential homeowners also could learn of designs before they ever contacted a builder, by perusing catalogues and magazines or talking with friends or colleagues who had used published designs. Definitive proof of who actually selected the designs used in Waxahachie is missing; but, at least with the Barber designs, it appears likely that the homeowners initiated their use more often than builders did. Most of the owners were linked by professional, social, or geographical situations that would have facilitated exchange of information about published design sources. Then as now, people were likely to look around their towns and neighborhoods and talk to their friends and colleagues when they contemplated building. This influence by example and word of mouth played an important role in the dissemination and acceptance of published designs.

Waxahachie benefited from the use of published designs for its houses. The surviving houses based on published designs are among the architectural treasures of the town, along with the red granite and sandstone courthouse, designed by J. Reily Gordon in 1895, that dominates the town's square (see Waxahachie map). Even before the preservation movement of the 1960s and 1970s reached Waxahachie, these houses served as reminders of the vision and pride of their original owners. In late-nineteenth-century Waxahachie, as in most of Texas, using published designs evidently was an acceptable method by which potential homeowners could secure pleasing and stylish houses. The resulting houses were viewed as showplaces by the community when they were built and served as models or sources of inspiration for even more houses, extending the influence of the original published designs far beyond the original intentions or even the knowledge of their creators.

8

. . . . .

Conclusion

An impressive array of house designs in books, magazines, and catalogues was available to nineteenth- and early-twentieth-century Texans. As the examples in this book indicate, many of those designs served as sources of inspiration for Texas houses. Even though the number of examples presented here is too small to convey a full understanding of the impact of published house designs on Texas domestic architecture, these houses, along with data about their owners and builders, provide enough evidence not only to confirm the widespread use of published designs, but also to indicate the variety of situations in which they were used.

The impact of published house designs on Texas domestic architecture went far beyond those instances in which designs were borrowed in their entirety—the focus of this book. Published designs also served as sources of ideas that local designers and potential homeowners could extract and combine in ways never imagined by their original creators. One example of such a practice has been preserved in the papers of Galveston resident Josephine Mason Scrimgeour, although the house she planned appears never to have been built. Mrs. Scrimgeour designed her dream house by choosing pieces from a variety of published sources and writing notes about how they should be altered and combined. She selected a door from a house design by architect A. Raymond Ellis, published in the magazine *Woman's Home Companion;* and a roof and dormers from other magazines and newspapers.[1] Architects, carpenter-builders, and individuals all probably borrowed design elements and details from published sources when planning houses.

As the example of Mrs. Scrimgeour indicates, published design sources also contributed to increased consumer awareness and concern about architectural styles and house plans. Pattern books, magazines, and mail-order catalogues bombarded the general public with house designs and encouraged readers to become actively involved in the planning and design of their own homes. In addition, some of the sources, such as the designs in *Godey's Lady's Book* and *Woman's Home Companion,* were directed specifically toward women, and others were advertised in women's magazines.

Fig. 153. *Hufsmith House, 207 S Magnolia St., Palestine, built 1901; significantly altered in later years. Photo from W. W. Dexter,* Texas: Imperial State of America with Her Diadem of Cities. *Reproduction courtesy University of Houston Libraries.*

Fig. 154. *Design No. 24, George F. Barber,* Modern Dwellings, *3d ed., p. 159.*

With such encouragement, many Texas women, including Jane Field Jones, Rebecca Brown, and Emma Patrick, became involved in the design selection of their homes.

Building a house based on a published design appears to have been a practice that was socially and culturally acceptable during this period. We have seen, beginning with the Browns in Galveston, that many prosperous and respected Texans took advantage of published designs. The resulting houses were admired in their time and often were touted in promotional literature as prime examples of residential architecture. As an example, Dexter's book, *Texas: Imperial State of America*, which was published for distribution at the 1904 Saint Louis

Exposition, included an illustration of the Trippet House in Waxahachie (then owned by J. S. Skinner) and another of the house in Palestine owned by Frank Hufsmith, "one of the best citizens of Texas." Both houses happened to be based on published designs (figs. 153 and 154).[2]

Unfortunately, during the twentieth century, a stigma became attached to the use of published designs, particularly those in mail-order catalogues.[3] It should be evident from many of the examples in this book, however, that the use of published designs was not inherently a bad thing. The quality of a design is not altered through the process of publication; in truth, in the nineteenth and early twentieth centuries, it was possible to obtain better designs from the printed page than from many local designers.

Both published and locally produced designs inevitably varied in quality. The designs, as well as the houses built from them, reflect architectural trends and styles, along with the strengths and weaknesses of their individual creators. Good, bad, and simply mediocre house designs were published; but, luckily, not every design published actually was built. Texans chose the designs they preferred from the myriad available. For the most part, they seem to have managed to avoid the worst examples.

Pattern books, magazines, and house catalogues were only parts of a web including published designs, technological developments, existing structures, and client expectations. This complex of publications, technology, and consumerism affected the producers of published designs, as well as local designers. What designers did with the resources at their disposal is an important measure of their accomplishment, and we cannot truly understand that accomplishment until we increase our knowledge of those resources.

This book has addressed one component of the web of design influences: published house designs. The houses illustrated here attest to the direct influence of published designs. Once built, they in turn influenced other designs through their presence in the built environment. They also became part of the complex of material, social, cultural, and technical elements that contributed to the world of our ancestors and that forms part of our heritage.

Houses built from published designs also, quite often, gave pleasure to their owners, their neighbors, and passersby. Many of the houses that have survived continue to provide us with enjoyment, even as they serve as witnesses to the aspirations of their owners and the abilities of their designers and builders.

Notes

Previously published information about these houses ranges from an entire book, in the case of Ashton Villa, to nothing at all, for many others. The notes below document both the published and unpublished sources used in determining construction dates and other background information about the houses and their owners and builders. However, two types of sources have not been given full bibliographic citations within the notes: city directories and the U.S. Population Census Schedules.

When city directories are available, they can be used to determine approximate construction dates and original owners' names and occupations, although their information is not always reliable. The search process involves checking the address indexes of many volumes over the range of years when a house might have been constructed and then checking the names listings for the names given. I have not cited the publisher and exact title of each directory consulted, since, in most large collections, they are arranged and accessed simply by city, then date. The major city directory collections that I consulted were in the Texas and Local History Department of the Houston Public Library and the Center for American History at the University of Texas at Austin.

The U.S. Population Census Schedules are archival records available on microfilm that provide the data collected by census-takers about each household. The records are useful in obtaining background information about owners and builders and can sometimes be used to confirm information found in city directories. For the years 1850 through 1920, but excluding 1890, which was destroyed by fire, the census data includes names, ages, occupations, and relationships of all members of a household. (The 1930 through 1990 censuses are all closed to public viewing.) Microfilm of all the available schedules for all Texas counties is held by the Clayton Genealogical Library of the Houston Public Library and at the Genealogy Collection of the Texas State Library in Austin. The genealogy collections of many local libraries contain the census microfilm for their counties.

Introduction

1. "What People Say of American Homes," *American Homes* 14, no. 1 (Jan. 1902): inside front cover.

2. Biographical information on Jane Field Jones is derived from Ida Campbell, *Oh, Strange New World*, 125–39; A. C. Jones obituary, *Beeville (Tex.) Bee Picayune*, Mar. 6, 1980; Jeanne Jones Hause, interview by Margaret Culbertson, Beeville, Tex., Dec. 16, 1996; Burt Hause and Jeanne Hause, *The Interview* [by Kathleen Jones Alexander], 10–12.

3. Jones House, 611 E. Jones St., built 1906: Nancy Goebel, "Pluck of the Irish," *Texas Homes* 9, no. 7 (July 1985): 51–53. Barber's design, "Residence on Missionary Ridge, Tenn.," is in *American Homes* 3, no. 5 (Nov. 1896): 150–51; and 10, no. 1 (Jan. 1900): 17, 20. The Jones House

in Beeville was brought to my attention by Michael A. Tomlan. Mrs. Jones also may have been involved in the design decision when her stepson, William W. Jones, a cattle rancher and financial entrepreneur, built an imposing Neoclassical mansion in Corpus Christi (511 S. Broadway, demolished). It bore a strong resemblance to another George Barber design, "Suburban Villa," in George F. Barber, *Modern Dwellings*, 5th ed., 196–97.

4. Works on the use of published design sources include James L. Garvin, "Mail-Order House Plans and American Victorian Architecture," *Winterthur Portfolio* 16, no. 4 (Winter 1981): 309–34; Dell Upton, "Pattern Books and Professionalism," *Winterthur Portfolio* 19, nos. 2–3 (1984): 107–50; Michael A. Tomlan, "Popular and Professional American Architectural Literature in the Late Nineteenth Century," Ph.D. diss., Cornell Univ., 1983; Alan Gowans, *The Comfortable House: North American Suburban Architecture, 1890–1930*; Sally McMurry, *Families and Farmhouses in Nineteenth-Century America*; Clay Lancaster, "Builders' Guide and Plan Books and American Architecture," *Magazine of Art* 61 (Jan. 1948): 16–22; Robert Schweitzer and Michael W. R. Davis, *America's Favorite Homes: Mail-Order Catalogues as a Guide to Popular Early–20th-Century Houses*; Herbert Gottfried and Jan Jennings, *American Vernacular Design: 1870–1940*; Michael J. Crosbie, "From 'Cookbooks' to 'Menus': The Transformation of Architecture Books in Nineteenth-Century America," *Material Culture* 17 (1985): 1–23; Robert P. Guter and Janet W. Foster, *Building by the Book: Pattern-Book Architecture in New Jersey*; Daniel D. Reiff, "Identifying Mail-Order and Catalog Houses," *Old-House Journal* 23, no. 5 (Sept.–Oct. 1995): 30–37.

5. The most substantial work on domestic architecture in Texas is Drury Blakley Alexander, *Texas Homes of the Nineteenth Century*, which features the following houses that since publication have been discovered to be based on published designs: J. M. Brown House (Ashton Villa) in Galveston, House at 407 East Main Street in Clarksville, Ike West House in San Antonio, House at 710 Houston St. in Crockett, Parish-Jones House in Calvert (referred to simply as "A Victorian House, Calvert"), and John Bremond House in Austin. Among the earliest attributions of Texas houses to specific published designs were the Parrish House in Calvert, with its Barber source, in "Our Correspondents," *Old-House Journal* 7, no. 12 (Dec. 1980): 193; and the Downes-Aldrich House in Crockett and the Parish-

Jones House in Calvert, with their Barber sources, in James Wright Steely, *A Catalog of Texas Properties in the National Register of Historic Places*, 105 and 149. Multiple examples were included in Margaret Culbertson and Ellen Beasley, "Use of Published House Plans for Domestic Architecture in Texas: 1890–1930," unpub. report submitted to Texas Society of Architects, Austin, 1986. Some of those examples appeared in later publications: Joe Nick Patoski, with research by Margaret Culbertson, "Houses by Number," *Domain: The Lifestyle Magazine of Texas Monthly* (Summer 1988): 20–24; Margaret Culbertson, "From Mail House to Your House: Catalogue Sources of Houston Domestic Architecture, 1880–1930," *Cite: The Architecture and Design Review of Houston*, no. 24 (Spring 1990): 22–23; Margaret Culbertson, "Mail-Order Mansions: Catalogue Sources of Domestic Architecture in North Central Texas," *Legacies: A History Journal for Dallas and North Central Texas* 4, no. 2 (Fall 1992): 8–20. Examples from Culbertson, "Mail House to Your House," were included in Barrie Scardino, "The Development of Domestic Architecture," in Dorothy Knox Howe Houghton et al., *Houston's Forgotten Heritage*. The Harris House in Fort Worth, with its *Craftsman* source, was included in Carol Roark, *Fort Worth's Legendary Landmarks*, 96–97. Kenneth Hafertepe presents a published design by Samuel Sloan as the probable source of Ashton Villa in his book, *History of Ashton Villa*, but the design presented later in this book is a more likely source. Elizabeth Skidmore Sasser, *Dugout to Deco: Building in West Texas, 1880–1930*, lists some of the books and catalogues that were available to Texas builders (pp. 56–57) and gives the George Barber source of the Barton House, now located at the Ranching Heritage Center at Lubbock; but she also includes, without sources, at least two other houses that were based on published designs: the house at 611 Coggin Avenue in Brownwood and the bungalow at 1816 Hurley in Fort Worth.

6. Books, journals, and surveys consulted include the following: Drury Alexander, *Texas Homes*; Dorothy K. Bracken, *Early Texas Homes*; Willard B. Robinson, *Gone from Texas: Our Lost Architectural Heritage*; Jay C. Henry, *Architecture in Texas, 1895–1945*; *Historic American Buildings: Texas*; Steely, *Catalog of Texas Properties*; Virginia and Lee McAlester, *A Field Guide to American Houses*; *Endangered Historic Properties of Texas*; Ann Ruff, *Historic Homes of Texas*; Sasser, *Dugout to Deco*; William Lloyd McDonald, *Dallas Rediscovered: A*

Photographic Chronicle of Urban Expansion, 1870–1925;
A Guide to the Older Neighborhoods of Dallas; Houghton
et al., *Houston's Forgotten Heritage;* Drexel Turner et al.,
Houston Architectural Survey, 6 vols.; Stephen Fox,
Houston Architectural Guide; Austin Chapter, AIA,
*Austin and Its Architecture; Austin: Its Architects and
Architecture (1836–1986);* Roxanne Kuter Williamson,
Austin, Texas: An American Architectural History; San
Antonio Chapter, the AIA, *Guide to San Antonio
Architecture;* Mary V. Burkholder, *Down the Acequia
Madre in the King William Historic District;* Mary V.
Burkholder, *The King William Area: A History and Guide
to the Houses,* 2d ed; Ellen Beasley and Stephen Fox,
Galveston Architecture Guidebook; Howard Barnstone,
The Galveston That Was; Lavonia Jenkins Barnes, *Early
Homes of Waco, and the People Who Lived in Them;
Portals at the Pass; Texas Homes, 1979–87;* Jay C. Henry
et al., "Residential Design in Typical American Architec-
ture: The Swiss Avenue District, 1905–1932," *Perspective*
10, no. 1 (1981): 17–22; Historic Preservation Council for
Tarrant County, *Tarrant County Historic Resources
Survey: Fort Worth: Upper North, Northeast, East, Far
South, and Far West;* Historic Preservation Council for
Tarrant County, *Tarrant County Historic Resources
Survey: Phase III, Fort Worth's Southside;* Ellen Beasley
and Wellborn, *Abilene, Texas: Preservation Survey and
Plan, 1979,* prepared for the Planning and Community
Development Department, City of Abilene, and the
Texas Historical Commission, printed by the City of
Abilene, Mar., 1979; Ellen Beasley, *Investment in Tradi-
tion: Preservation Plan for Hillsboro, Texas,* prepared for
the Hillsboro Heritage League, Inc., and the Texas
Historical Commission, Apr., 1982; Ellen Beasley,
*Historic Preservation Survey and Plan for Wichita Falls,
Texas,* prepared for the Wichita County Heritage
Society, May, 1982; Ellen Beasley, *Orange, Texas: Preser-
vation Plan,* prepared for the City of Orange, Dec., 1977;
and Dan K. Utley, ed., *Sentimental Journey: A Guide to
Preserving the Architectural Heritage of Georgetown,
Texas.* Numerous county and local histories were also
scanned for likely houses.

7. The most substantial collection of house-design
sources probably is at the Library of Congress, but many
other libraries around the country contain important
items and collections. For a list of the libraries consulted
for this book, see the acknowledgments.

Chapter 1. Picking a Pattern

1. Doorway of the Nichols-Rice-Cherry House:
Historic American Buildings Survey (microform): Texas,
fiche no. 24, HABS no. 33-B-1; Jesse A. Ziegler, *Wave of
the Gulf,* 65; Harvin C. Moore, "The Restoration of the
Nichols-Rice House," *AIA Journal* 37, no. 1 (Jan. 1962):
28; Scardino, "Development of Domestic Architecture,"
69, 192; Minard Lafever, *Modern Builder's Guide,* plate
63. The design detail on the outside pilasters is similar to
that on the pilasters in plate 29 of Asher Benjamin,
Practice of Architecture. Other doorways similar to
Lafever's design can be found at Waveland (the Joseph
Bryan House), Lexington, Ky., and the Charles Kerrison
House, Charleston, S.C.

2. Sources on the influence of builders guides in
Texas include Drury Alexander, *Texas Homes,* 87; Gus
Hamblett, "The 'Plain Style:' Some Sources for the
Greek Revival in Texas," *Texas Architect* 36, no. 3 (May–
June 1986): 60–69; and Kenneth Hafertepe, *Abner Cook:
Master Builder on the Texas Frontier.*

3. Tomlan, "Popular and Professional American
Architectural Literature," refers to the publications of
Downing and his followers as "style manuals" and the
post–Civil-War publications of Bicknell, Woodward,
etc., as "pattern books." The distinctions of this terminology are useful, but in this book I follow the more
common terminology, which refers to all non–mail-
order-catalogue books that present house designs as
pattern books. The definitions in Ward Bucher's
Dictionary of Building Preservation and James Stevens
Curl's *Encyclopaedia of Architectural Terms* support this
usage.

4. Andrew Jackson Downing, *Cottage Residences,* ix.

5. A few of the many sources on Downing include
David Schuyler, *Apostle of Taste: Andrew Jackson
Downing, 1815–1852;* Dumbarton Oaks Colloquium on
the History of Landscape Architecture (11th), *Prophet
with Honor: The Career of Andrew Jackson Downing,
1815–1852;* and Adam W. Sweeting, *Reading Houses and
Building Books: Andrew Jackson Downing and the
Architecture of Popular Literature, 1835–1855.*

6. One example is an announcement about the
September issue of *Godey's Lady's Book* in the *Bellville
(Tex.) Countryman,* Aug. 25, 1860, p. 3.

7. The greatest concentration of published information on Ashton Villa and the Brown family is in Hafertepe, *History of Ashton Villa.* Hafertepe presents plate 88

from Samuel Sloan, *The Model Architect,* as Ashton Villa's design source, but I feel that the design published in *Godey's* is more convincing. Ashton Villa is included in several other sources, including Beasley and Fox, *Galveston Architecture Guidebook,* 56–57; Barnstone, *Galveston That Was,* 55–63; and Drury Alexander, *Texas Homes,* 198, 258–59.

8. Frank L. Mott, *History of American Magazines, 1741–1850,* 581.

9. Louis Godey, "Godey's Arm Chair," *Godey's Lady's Book* 77, no. 461 (1868): 456.

10. George L. Hersey, "Godey's Choice," *Journal of the Society of Architectural Historians* 18, no. 3 (Oct. 1959): 104–11.

11. Scardino, "Development of Domestic Architecture," 72. The only surviving visual record of the house is a woodcut on the *Wood Map of Houston,* dated 1869, in the collection of the Texas and Local History Department of the Houston Public Library.

12. Sources on Orson Squire Fowler include Tomlan, "Popular and Professional American Architectural Literature," 85–87; Guter and Foster, *Building by the Book,* 120; Madeleine B. Sterne, "Introduction to the Dover Edition," in *The Octagon House: A Home for All,* by Orson S. Fowler (originally published as *A Home for All*), v–xii; Walter Creese, "Fowler and the Domestic Octagon," *Art Bulletin* 28 (June 1946): 89–102.

13. "Octagonal Country Seat of O. S. Fowler," *Godey's Lady's Book* 49 (Oct. 1854): 336–38.

14. *Galveston Weekly News,* Mar. 8, 1859.

15. Henry A. Page, "Design for an Octagon House," *Horticulturist* 4, no. 11 (May 1850): 516–18 and frontispiece.

16. Sadie Gwin Blackburn, "The Evolution of the Houston Landscape," in Houghton et al., *Houston's Forgotten Heritage,* 22–23.

17. Peter Flagg Maxson, "The Octagon Option in Texas," *Perspective* 9 (Dec. 1980): 14–17.

18. House at 407 East Main Street, Clarksville, originally built ca. 1880 for a "Dr. Look," according to Byron Black to Margaret Culbertson, June 17, 1996, author's collection. The 1880 U.S. Population Census Schedules for Red River County list an E. S. Look, occupation physician, living in Clarksville with his wife and two sons. The house is illustrated in Drury Alexander, *Texas Homes,* 199 and 259, but no information about owner, builder, or date of construction is given.

19. E. C. Hussey, *Home Building,* plate 14.

20. A. J. Bicknell, *The Specimen Book of 100 Architectural Designs* (New York: A. J. Bicknell and Company, 1878), 15. Sources on Bicknell's publications include: Tomlan, "Popular and Professional American Architectural Literature"; Paul Goeldner, "New Introduction and Commentary," in *Bicknell's Village Builder and Supplement,* by A. J. Bicknell & Co.; and Guter and Foster, *Building by the Book,* 123–28.

21. John Bremond House, 700 Guadalupe St., Austin: John C. Garner, Jr., "John Bremond House, Photographs and Written Historical and Descriptive Data," *Historic American Buildings Survey,* TEX-3140, p. 2; Drury Alexander, *Texas Homes,* 217, 261; Williamson, *Austin, Texas,* 105–107; Austin Chapter, AIA, *Austin and Its Architecture,* 14; *Austin: Its Architects and Architecture,* 38–39.

22. The shingle pattern of the roof resembles that in supplementary plate 9, and the masonry band linking the second-floor windows repeats details from the courthouse design on plates 49 and 50. Bicknell & Co., *Bicknell's Village Builder,* plates 49–50 and supplementary plates 2, 9, and 11, unpaged.

23. Isaac Hobbs, *Hobbs's Architecture,* dedication page.

24. Smith M. Ellis House, also known as the Ike West House, 422 King William St., San Antonio: Burkholder, *King William Area,* 53; San Antonio Chapter, AIA, *Guide to San Antonio Architecture,* 72; Drury Alexander, *Texas Homes,* 201, 259. Hobbs, *Hobbs's Architecture,* 188–89; and Isaac Hobbs, *Godey's Lady's Book* 92 (Feb. 1876): 196.

25. Hobbs, *Hobbs's Architecture,* 188.

26. House at 710 Houston St., Crockett (demolished): illustrated in Drury Alexander, *Texas Homes,* 194 and 258, but no information about owner, builder, or date of construction is given. A construction date of 1900–1901 and original owner C. C. Warfield are given in Eliza H. Bishop to Margaret Culbertson, Nov. 19, 1997, author's collection. A construction date of 1890s is given in *Old Homes of Houston County, Texas,* 169. An earlier construction date and original owner are a strong possibility worth investigating. Hobbs, *Hobbs's Architecture,* 74–75, and *Godey's Lady's Book* 82 (Feb. 1871): 201.

27. House for Charles S. House, originally located at 1806 Main St., built 1882, demolished ca. 1920: Scardino, "Development of Domestic Architecture," 81, 129. Design No. 1, in Hobbs, *Hobbs's Architecture,* 22–23; and *Godey's Lady's Book* 82 (June 1871): 580.

28. Hobbs, *Hobbs's Architecture,* 21.

Chapter 2. Victorian Variety

1. Henry W. Cleaveland et al., *Village and Farm Cottages*, [viii].

2. Background sources on the Pallisers include Jeff Wilkinson, "Who They Were: Geo. Palliser," *Old-House Journal* 18, no. 6 (Nov.–Dec. 1990): 18–20; Gery E. French, "Letters: Palliser Pedigree," *Old-House Journal* 19, no. 4 (July–Aug. 1991): 8, 10; Michael A. Tomlan, "The Palliser Brothers and Their Publications," introduction in *Palliser's Late Victorian Architecture*, by Palliser, Palliser & Co., reprint ed., unpaged; Guter and Foster, *Building by the Book*, 151–55.

3. Palliser, Palliser and Co., New York, to T. Gonzales, Galveston, June 4, 1886, in Gonzales Family Papers, Rosenberg Library, Galveston.

4. *Galveston Evening Standard*, Apr. 2, 1887.

5. Cotton House, 1018 Travis St., demolished: Scardino, "Development of Domestic Architecture," 86, 150; Culbertson, "Mail House to Your House," 22–23.

6. Tomlan, "Popular and Professional American Architectural Literature," 315–37.

7. Dillingham House, 1214 Rusk Ave., Houston, demolished: Scardino, "Development of Domestic Architecture," 86, 90–91, 150–51; Culbertson, "Mail House to Your House," 22–23; Design 485 in *Shoppell's Modern Houses* 2, no. 2 (Aug. 1887): 18.

8. The Adams, Robinson, and Price letters appeared in *Shoppell's Modern Houses* 4, no. 2 (Jan. 1890): 63. The client names from Denison, El Paso, etc., were published on the last page (unnumbered) of Robert W. Shoppell, *Modern Houses, Beautiful Homes*. These letters and names were repeated in other issues of *Shoppell's Modern Houses* and other catalogues. The builders' names were published under the heading "Testimony of Practical Men" in *Shoppell's Modern Houses* 3, no. 2 (Jan. 1889): 48.

9. David S. Hopkins, *Houses and Cottages*, [ii].

10. George F. Barber, *New Model Dwellings*, 5.

11. Advertisement for Herbert C. Chivers, *Artistic Homes* (1901 ed.), in *Ladies' Home Journal* 18, no. 4 (Mar. 1901): 46. Advertisement for Chivers, *Artistic Homes* (1910 ed.), in *Country Life in America* 17, no. 6 (Apr. 1910): 662.

12. Herbert C. Chivers, *Artistic Homes*, 166 (Butler letter), 854 (Leonard letter), 837 (McInnis letter), and 839 (Gage letter).

13. "Thornburg Residence," in Chivers, *Artistic Homes*, 416. Becker House, 1130 S. Henderson St., Fort Worth, ca. 1906, no longer extant: Historic Preservation Council for Tarrant County, *Tarrant County Historic Resources Survey: Phase III, Fort Worth's Southside*, 32.

14. Navarro County Mechanic's Liens (Jan. 16, 1907), 4:522, Navarro County Courthouse, Corsicana, Texas.

15. Sandra L. Tatman, *Biographical Dictionary of Philadelphia Architects, 1700–1930*, 393.

16. Jan Jennings, "Leila Ross Wilburn: Plan-Book Architect," *Women's Art Journal* 10 (Spring–Summer 1989): 10–16.

17. *Dallas Morning News*, Jan. 20, 1910.

18. Associated Architects, *Fifty House Plans Designed for Home Builders in the Southwest*, 4.

19. Ibid., 26. Background on the development of Munger Place and the construction date of 1909 for 5019 Tremont in National Register of Historic Places Inventory—Nomination Form, Munger Place Historic District, 1978, available at the Texas Historical Commission, Austin.

20. Ibid., 3.

Chapter 3. Mail-Order Master

1. "Description of Designs and Plans," *American Homes* 4, no. 2 (Feb. 1897): 42.

2. T. W. Trout House, 705 Poplar, Honey Grove: Steely, *Catalog of Texas Properties*, 58; Nancy Goebel, "Historic Homes," *Texas Homes* 9, no. 1 (Jan. 1985): 73–83; "In North Carolina Mountains," *American Homes* 5, no. 1 (July 1897): 8–9, 12.

3. Design No. 263, Barber, *Modern Dwellings*, 5th ed., also published with the title "With a Complete Attic," in *American Homes* 12, no. 2 (Feb. 1901): 78–79. Saul House, originally built for the Saul family on a farm in the country south of Hutto in 1905–1906, and later moved to site near Coupland: Susan M. Ridgway, "Old-House Living in Central Texas," *Old-House Journal* 10, no. 11 (Nov. 1982): 223–26; and Susan Ridgway to Margaret Culbertson, June 3, 1986, author's collection. This example was first brought to my attention by Richard Lucier. Holland House, 803 N. Sixth St., Orange, built ca. 1910 for George E. Holland: Curtis F. Jeanis to Margaret Culbertson, Jan. 3, 1998, author's collection. J. N. Donohoo House, southwest corner of 7th and Columbia Sts., Plainview, built ca. 1907, moved in the late 1950s to an unknown location: Vera Dean Wofford, *Hale County: Facts and Folklore*, 494–96.

4. Sources on Barber's life and work include Michael A. Tomlan, "Toward the Growth of an Artistic Taste," in *Cottage Souvenir No. 2*, by George F. Barber, reprint ed., 4–19; Charles Hite-Smith, "Plans and Plan-making," *American Homes* 2, no. 1 (Jan. 1896): 22–25; and Barber's obituary, *Knoxville Journal and Tribune*, Feb. 18, 1915.

5. Tomlan, "Toward Growth of Artistic Taste," 6.

6. *Inland Architect* 9, no. 10 (July 1887): 100, and *Inland Architect* 11, no. 8 (July 1888): 91. "House Design," *Carpentry and Building* 10, no. 3 (Mar. 1888): 50–54, and "Residence of W. G. Earle," *Carpentry and Building* 10, no. 11 (Nov. 1888): 226 and plates 42–43.

7. "Trade Notes," *Carpentry and Building* 10, no. 12 (Dec. 1888): 268.

8. George F. Barber, *Cottage Souvenir No. 2*, 6.

9. "General Book Notices," *Builder and Woodworker* (Feb. 1889): 32.

10. Barber, *Cottage Souvenir No. 2*, 88–89, 121.

11. Tomlan, "Toward Growth of Artistic Taste," 12.

12. Haden House, 603 W. Bonham St., Ladonia: Steely, *Catalog of Texas Properties*, 58. As of April 29, 1997, information and photographs of the house were mounted on the owner's home page: LeAnne Davis, "The Davis Dungeon," http://www.geocities.com/Heartland/Plains/1894/haden/html. Coleman House, originally located in the 900 block of East Tyler St., Athens: Henderson County Historical Commission, *Old Homes of Henderson County*, 33.

13. The *Map of Houston Heights*, with woodcut illustrations, was published in at least two undated versions. One is in the Special Collections, Univ. of Houston Libraries, and the other is in the Heights Branch, Houston Public Library. The Houston Public Library version was reprinted in Sister Mary Agatha, *History of Houston Heights, 1891–1918*. The following are the houses shown on the Houston Public Library version and the designs from Barber, *Cottage Souvenir No. 2*, to which they are related: "Residence on Boulevard, between 15th and 16th Aves." (Mills House), Design No. 56; "Residence on Boulevard, between 8th and 9th Aves.," Design No. 1; "Residence on Boulevard, corner 11th Ave." (Milroy House), Design No. 30; "Cottage, Corner 16th Ave. and Rutland Street," Design No. 2; "Residence, Corner 18th Ave. and Harvard Street" (Mansfield House), Design No. 30. Culbertson, "Mail House to Your House," 22–23. Milroy House and Mansfield House: Fox, *Houston Architectural Guide*, 188–89.

14. *American Homes* 14, no. 1 (Jan. 1902) and 14, no. 2 (Feb. 1902): both, inside front cover (unnumbered).

15. *American Homes* 1, no. 3 (Sept. 1895): 85, 112; and *American Homes* 3, no. 2 (Aug. 1896): 48–49.

16. K. D. Lawrence House, Noble St., Lovelady, built ca. 1899: Armistead A. Aldrich, *History of Houston County, Texas*, 65; *Old Homes of Houston County, Texas*, 86. George F. Barber, *Art in Architecture*, 2d ed., Design No. 582. Same design also in *American Homes* 5, no. 3 (Sept. 1897): 81. Gabled balcony also in *American Homes* 12, no. 2 (Feb. 1901): 87.

17. *American Homes* 12, no. 2 (Feb. 1901): 80.

18. George O. Garnsey, *American Glossary of Architectural Terms*, gives the following definition: "Cottage—Generally applied to a small dwelling." The descriptive text in Barber, *Cottage Souvenir No. 2*, refers to the larger, two-story designs as "houses" and the smaller, two-story and one-story designs as "cottages."

19. Tomlan, "Toward Growth of Artistic Taste," 12, 19.

20. J. E. Downes House, 206 N. 7th St., Crockett: "Downes-Aldrich House, National Register of Historic Places Inventory—Nomination Form," 1977, available from Texas Historical Commission, Austin. This example was brought to my attention by Richard Lucier. E. A. Blount House, North St., Nacogdoches, no longer extant: Martha Anne Turner, *Old Nacogdoches in the Jazz Age*, 129–30.

21. "Stark House, 611 W. Green, Orange: Application Form for Official Texas Historical Marker" (Nov. 1, 1975), Nelda C. and H. J. Lutcher Stark Foundation, Orange, Texas; Steely, *Catalog of Texas Properties*, 141. The similarity of the Stark House carriage house to Barber's "City Barn," Design No. 95B in his *New Model Dwellings*, supports the probable Barber source for the Stark House design.

22. Powell House, Waxahachie, no longer extant, is discussed in more detail in ch. 7. Barthold House, 308 W. Couts, Weatherford, 1895, exterior alterations over the years: *American Homes* 1, no. 3 (Sept. 1895): 85, 112; and *American Homes* 3, no. 2 (Aug. 1896): 48–49; "Weatherford," *Texas Homes* 6, no. 3 (Apr. 1982): 28. Mills House, 1530 Heights Boulevard, Houston, built 1893, demolished: Scardino, "Development of Domestic Architecture," 86, 149.

23. Parish-Jones House, 609 Gregg St., Calvert, 1898: Drury Alexander, *Texas Homes*, 213, 260, illustrated but lacking the Barber attribution; Linda Montgomery, "Calvert," *Texas Homes* 4, no. 2 (Mar. 1980): 83; "Our

Correspondent," *Old-House Journal* 8, no. 12 (Dec. 1980): 193; Steely, *Catalog of Texas Properties*, 149. "Design No. 27," in Barber, *Cottage Souvenir, Revised and Enlarged*, 61, was also included in Barber, *Artistic Homes: How to Plan and How to Build Them*, 13.

24. "Artistic Colonial Home," *American Homes* 2, no. 1 (Jan. 1896): 3, also published in Barber, *Modern Dwellings*, 3d ed., 107. Lambertson House, 611 Coggin Avenue, Brownwood, built ca. 1901: "Heritage Homes" (calendar), and illustrated in Sasser, *Dugout to Deco*, 66–67. (This example was contributed by Michael Alcorn.) Waddell House, 2404 Caroline Ave., Houston, ca. 1901, demolished: Culbertson, "Mail House to Your House," 22–23; Scardino, "Development of Domestic Architecture," 92, 154.

25. Hackney House, 2210 Main St., Houston, 1903, demolished: Culbertson, "Mail House to Your House," 22–23; Scardino, "Development of Domestic Architecture," 95, 169. Rhode House, Bryan, demolished 1965: *A Better Day Is Dawning: History of the First One Hundred Years of the First Baptist Church of Bryan, Texas*, 50–51.

26. Westfall House, 393 Hawthorne St., Houston, 1905; Drexel Turner et al., *Houston Architectural Survey*, 4:852–54; Culbertson, "Mail House to Your House," 22–23;

27. "Follows Wife to the Beyond," *Knoxville Journal and Tribune*, Feb. 18, 1915.

Chapter 4. Myriad of Magazines

1. Navarro County Mechanic's Liens (Nov. 6, 1922), vol. 7.

2. Gwendolyn Wright, *Moralism and the Model Home*, 136–49.

3. *Godey's Lady's Book* 100 (Feb. 1880): 184; U.S. Bureau of the Census, Records for Duval County, 1880.

4. *National Builder* 16, no. 4 (Apr. 1893): 78–79. I have not been able to discover the original addresses of these houses.

5. *National Builder* 29, no. 6 (Dec. 1899) 8–9, and *National Builder* 34, no. 1 (Jan. 1902): 24. I have not been able to discover the original addresses of these houses.

6. "Residency of W. G. Earle," *Carpentry and Building* 10, no. 11 (Nov. 1888): 226, plates 42 and 43. Clendenen House, 803 N. Main St., Bonham: Steely, *Catalog of Texas Properties*, 57.

7. *Beaumont (Tex.) Enterprise*, Nov. 2, 9, 16, and 30, 1889.

8. "Dwelling at Waterbury, Conn.," *Scientific American, Architects' and Builders' Edition* 32, no. 3 (Sept. 1901): 49, 55.

9. U.S. Bureau of the Census, Records for Harris County, 1910; Houston city directories, 1907, 1908–1909, 1912.

10. 1348 Heights Boulevard, Houston, originally located across the street and moved in 1991. Barber and Klutz, "Design A181, A Compact Modern House," *Keith's Magazine on Home Building* 16, no. 3 (Sept. 1906): 162.

11. "A Craftsman House: Series of 1904, Number One," *Craftsman* 5, no. 4 (Jan. 1904): 399, and, announcing that the practice would stop, "Important Announcement," *Craftsman* 13, no. 1 (Oct. 1907), xi–xii.

12. *Craftsman* 16, no. 4 (July 1909): 456–63; Gustav Stickley, *More Craftsman Homes*, 70–71. Harris House, 4621 Foard St., Fort Worth: Culbertson, "Mail-Order Mansions," 16–17; Historic Preservation Council for Tarrant County, *Tarrant County Historic Resources Survey: Fort Worth: Upper North, Northeast, East, Far South, and Far West*, 170; Roark, *Fort Worth's Legendary Landmarks*, 96–97. I learned of this example through Ellen Beasley.

13. Feldman House, 1105 Prospect, El Paso: "Craftsman House: Series of 1905, Number VII," *Craftsman* 8, no. 4 (July 1905): 535–43; "A House of Craftsman Ideas," *Craftsman* 13, no. 5 (Feb. 1908): 572–77; "Craftsman House in Texas," *Craftsman* 21, no. 1 (Oct. 1911): 85–88. The house still exists in good condition, but it has been repainted to reverse the original light and dark patterns.

14. "Craftsman House in Texas," *Craftsman* 21, no. 1 (Oct. 1911): 85.

15. *Craftsman* 8, no. 3 (May 1905): xxxii.

16. "Cottage of Moderate Cost," *Farm and Ranch* 20, no. 46 (Nov. 16, 1901): 13, and "Six Room Cottage," *Farm and Ranch* 21, no. 45 (Nov. 8, 1902): 18. 2902 and 2906 Swiss Avenue, Dallas: Culbertson, "Mail-Order Mansions," 12–14; McDonald, *Dallas Rediscovered*, 132–33; Preservation Dallas, "A Visitor's Guide to the Wilson Historic District" (Dallas: Preservation Dallas, n.d.).

17. "Modern Southern Cottage," *Farm and Ranch* 20, no. 6 (Feb. 9, 1901): 18. 1813 K St., Plano; and 500 Magnolia St., Hubbard: Culbertson, "Mail-Order Mansions," 12–14. These two matches were contributed by Ellen Beasley.

18. Karen Collins, "Holland's Magazine," in Ron Tyler, ed., *New Handbook of Texas*, 3:666.

19. Plan No. 2007, *Holland's Magazine* (May 1920): 24.

Mitchell-Stuart House, 2812 Avenue D, Forth Worth: Historic Preservation Council for Tarrant County, *Tarrant County Historic Resources Survey: Fort Worth: Upper North, Northeast, East, Far South, and Far West,* 100; Culbertson, "Mail-Order Mansions," 14. 2228 Harrison, Fort Worth.

20. *Gulf Coast Lumberman* 4, no. 1 (Apr. 1, 1916): 16–17.

21. Plan No. 2522, in *Holland's Magazine* (June 1920): 22.

22. "Dignified by Its Simplicity," *San Antonio Light,* May 8, 1921; Charles Alma Byers, "Well-Planned and Attractive Stucco House," *Keith's Magazine on Home Building* 36, no. 6 (Dec. 1916): 385–88.

23. *Holland's Magazine* (Nov. 1918): 37. Harris House, 617 Fordyce, Blooming Grove. Evidently a typographical error was made in the mechanic's lien, for the house and plan match the design in the Nov. 1918 issue of *Holland's,* not the Nov. 1921 issue.

Chapter 5. Bungalows from Books

1. "Testimonials," *Bungalow Magazine* 1, no. 4 (June 1909).

2. Richard T. Bibb House, 1816 Hurley St., Fort Worth: illustration in Sasser, *Dugout to Deco,* 140. Approximate building date of 1912, owner's name, and occupation as manager of the S. T. Bibb Coal and Grain Co., from Fort Worth city directories, 1911 to 1922–23. Design No. 357, in Henry L. Wilson, *The Bungalow Book,* 4th ed., 66.

3. Sources on bungalows include Anthony D. King, *The Bungalow: The Production of a Global Culture,* 2d ed; Clay Lancaster, *The American Bungalow, 1880–1930;* Patricia Poore, "The Bungalow and Why We Love It So," *Old-House Journal* 13, no. 4 (May 1985): 90–93; and Robert Winter, *The California Bungalow.* Gowans, *Comfortable House,* 74–83.

4. Bungalow books published in 1906 include: E. E. Holman, *A Book of Bungalows;* and Frederick T. Hodgson, *Practical Bungalows and Cottages for Town and Country.*

5. "A Personal Talk about Stillwell Service," in E. W. Stillwell, *West Coast Bungalows,* [2].

6. Annie F. Johnston, *Mary Ware in Texas,* 25, 32–33.

7. "Finale," *Ye Planry Beautiful Homes.*

8. Stillwell, *West Coast Bungalows,* [2].

9. 1112 Drew St., Houston: "Design No. W-948," Stillwell, *West Coast Bungalows,* 48. Information on J. L. Jones from Harris County Deed Records, the classified

section of the *Houston Daily Post,* May 3, 1914, and Houston city directories for 1913, 1915, and 1917.

10. Standard Building Investment Co., *Standard Bungalows,* 36–37. 434 S. Chilton, Tyler: Smith County Mechanic's Liens (Mar. 20, 1922), 4:202, Smith County Courthouse, Tyler, Texas. This example contributed by Ellen Beasley. Information on L. E. Smith from U.S. Bureau of the Census, Records for Smith County, 1910.

11. 904 Ave. A, Santa Anna. E. W. Stillwell, *Representative California Homes,* 11.

12. 834 Iowa St., San Antonio, built ca. 1925, first owned by physician Charles A. Whittier, according to Fort Worth city directories, 1919 to 1927–28. Jud Yoho, *Craftsman Bungalows,* 8–9. Information about Yoho is in Dennis A. Andersen and Katheryn H. Krafft, "Pattern Books, Plan Books, Periodicals," in *Shaping Seattle Architecture,* ed. Jeffrey Karl Ochsner, 68–70.

13. Yoho, *Craftsman Bungalows,* 9.

14. G. S. Berry House, 1404 S. Adams St., Fort Worth, built 1907: Historic Preservation Council for Tarrant County, *Tarrant County Historic Resources Survey: Phase III: Fort Worth's Southside,* 131. Wilson, *Bungalow Book,* 14.

15. Wilson, *Bungalow Book,* 92–93.

16. Information on the Horton family from the Houston city directories for 1910–11 and 1912, and U.S. Bureau of the Census, Records for Harris County, 1910.

17. Information on Woodland Heights from "Woodland Heights," a promotional brochure published by the William A. Wilson Realty Co. in 1910; *Homes* (1911–12), a promotional magazine published by the William A. Wilson Co.; Mrs. W. G. Love, "Suburbs of Houston," in Mrs. Henry Fall, *The Key to the City of Houston,* 218–19; and William A. Wilson's obituary, *Houston Chronicle,* June 25, 1928.

18. J. J. Bruce House, 3215 Morrison, Houston: "What We Have Done for Others," *Homes* 2, no. 8 (Feb. 1912): 6–7, 10. Stillwell, *Representative California Homes,* 51. Information on Bruce family from Houston city directories, 1910–11, 1911–12, 1912, and 1913; and U.S. Bureau of the Census, Records for Harris County, 1910.

19. 3302 Beauchamp and 3301 Morrison illustrated and described in "Woodland Heights," 6, 11; and in "What We Have Done for Others," *Homes* (Mar. 1912): 6–7. Wilson, *Bungalow Book,* 62 and 886–87. Information about Ward family from the Houston city directories, 1910–11, 1911–12, 1912, and 1913; and U.S. Bureau of the Census, Records for Harris County, 1910. 4002

Austin illustrated in "What We Have Done for Others," *Homes* 2, no. 12 (June 1912): 6–7.

20. 3301 Houston Ave. illustrated and described in "Woodland Heights," 13. Wilson, *Bungalow Book,* 66.

21. Information on Rodney Horton family from U.S. Bureau of the Census, Records for Harris County, 1910.

22. *Ye Planry Bungalows,* 52–53.

23. "Woodland Heights," 19. Houston city directories, 1911–12 and 1912.

24. "Woodland Heights," *Suburbanite,* Sept. 12, 1908, p. 1. This citation and additional information on Irvin were discovered by Woodland Heights resident Ivon DuPont.

25. Houston city directories, 1908, 1910; U.S. Bureau of the Census, Records for Harris County, 1910. Irvin's obituary, *Houston Post,* Dec. 10, 1966.

26. *Gulf Coast Lumberman* 1, no. 22 (Feb. 15, 1914): 20.

27. *Ye Planry Beautiful Homes,* 2d page of foreword.

28. Ellis County Mechanic's Liens (Aug. 5, 1916), 7:164, Ellis County Courthouse, Waxahachie, Texas. "Homes for the Southwest," *Holland's Magazine* (June 1920): 22.

29. Corsicana Ye Planry houses, cited in Navarro County Mechanic's Liens (Nov. 6, 1922), 7:620. "Prospective Work," in *TGCA [Texas General Contractors Association] Monthly Bulletin* (May 1925): 24–26; (June 1925): 21; (July 1925): 20, 23; (Aug. 1925): 20, 23; (Sept. 1925): 20–21, 24; (Oct. 1925): 24; (Nov. 1925): 22.

30. "Telling Bungalow Plan No. 901," in George Palmer Telling, *Telling Plan Book, Spanish and Italian Bungalows.* Hicks House, 2400 Harrison Ave.: Historic Preservation Council for Tarrant County, *Tarrant County Historic Resources Survey: Phase III, Fort Worth's Southside,* 107.

31. *Homes of the Moment,* [4]. There is, unfortunately, no record of Mr. Hammer building a house for himself in El Paso.

Chapter 6. Ready-Made Residences

1. Sears, Roebuck and Co., *Modern Homes,* 93. The Carl House no longer exists.

2. *Galveston Daily News,* Dec. 28, 1866; and "Bangor Mechanics at the South," *Bangor Daily Whig and Courier,* Apr. 8, 1867. These citations were contributed by Ellen Beasley.

3. Examples of 19th-century ready-cut catalogues include D. N. Skilling and D. B. Flint, *Illustrated Cata-* logue of Portable Sectional Buildings Patented Nov. 19, 1861 (1863), and Ducker Portable House Co., *Illustrated Catalogue* (ca. 1888). Advertisements indicating the probable existence of catalogues include one for Ready-Made Houses of the Derrom Building Co. of Paterson, N.J., in *American Agriculturist* 31, no. 1 (Jan. 1872): 29, and for Ready-Made Houses by Lyman Bridges and Co. of New York City in *American Builder* 10 (1874), unpaged advertisement section. The 1908 Sears catalogue actually was intended to sell millwork, not entire houses, but the subsequent catalogues sold all of the building material pre-cut and ready to construct the houses. The history of Sears, Roebuck's production of ready-cut houses and catalogues is recounted in Katherine Cole Stevenson and H. Ward Jandl, *Houses by Mail: A Guide to Houses from Sears, Roebuck and Company.* Sears and other ready-cut companies are discussed in Schweitzer and Davis, *America's Favorite Homes,* and in Gowans, *Comfortable House,* 48–63, although Gowans incorrectly cites George Barber as a producer of mail-order houses. James C. Massey and Shirley Maxwell, "Pre-Cut Houses, 'Catalog Homes,'" *Old-House Journal* 18, no. 6 (Nov.–Dec. 1990): 36–41, treats various ready-cut house catalogues.

4. Bessie Patterson, *History of Deaf Smith County, Featuring Pioneer Families,* 76.

5. Sears, Roebuck and Co., *Modern Homes,* 10.

6. Stevenson and Jandl, *Houses by Mail,* 203.

7. *Aladdin Plan of Industrial Housing,* 2d ed., 4. Sears company housing is illustrated in Stevenson and Jandl, *Houses by Mail,* 23; and Sears, Roebuck, and Co., *Sears, Roebuck Catalog of Houses, 1926: An Unabridged Reprint,* 4–5.

8. Private collection of petroleum-industry archives.

9. Crain Ready-Cut House Co., *Ready-Cut and Sectional Houses, Catalogue No. 5,* 32–33.

10. Advertisement for Woodward and Hardie, Inc., Manufacturers of Ready Cut Houses, in San Antonio city directory, 1926, p. 156.

11. T. J. Williams, *Better Built Homes for Less Money,* 3–5.

12. *Gulf Coast Lumberman* 3, no. 13 (Oct. 1, 1915): 16.

13. Houses built in those cities were illustrated in the 1915 catalogue: Williams, *Better Built Homes for Less Money.* Sale of the company noted in *Houston Daily Post,* July 4, 1917.

14. Sources on E. L. Crain and the Crain Ready-Cut House Co. include: "Resolution of the Board of Directors, American General Insurance Company, on the

Death of Edward Lillo Crain," author's collection; Harry H. Steidle, "A Statement from the Prefabricated Home Manufacturers Association," *Arts + Architecture* 61, no. 7 (July 1944): 41–42; "Preview of a Post-war Prefabricated Home," *Prefabricated Homes* 3, no. 5 (Sept. 1944): 8–11, 24; Houston city directories, 1913 to 1930–31.

15. *Prefabricated Homes* 3, no. 5 (Sept. 1944): 24.

16. 1608 Haver St., built 1922: Harris County Deed Records and Houston city directories, 1922 and 1923. Design No. M-213, Crain Ready-Cut House Co., *Ready-Cut Homes, Catalog No. 4.*

17. *Gulf Coast Lumberman* 4, no. 9 (Aug. 1, 1916): 24; *Gulf Coast Lumberman* 4, no. 14 (Oct. 15, 1916): 41–43.

18. *Gulf Coast Lumberman* 5, no. 6 (June 15, 1917): 6.

19. *Gulf Coast Lumberman* 4, no. 10 (Aug. 15, 1916): 22.

20. *Gulf Coast Lumberman* 3, no. 18 (Dec. 15, 1915): 14.

21. *Gulf Coast Lumberman* 3, no. 15 (Nov. 1, 1915): 6, 9.

Chapter 7. Context of a Community

1. J. T. Cole, "Waxahachie," in W. W. Dexter, *Texas: Imperial State of America with Her Diadem of Cities.*

2. Biographical information on Oscar E. Dunlap and family: *Memorial and Biographical History of Ellis County,* 514; U.S. Bureau of the Census, Records for Ellis County, 1880 and 1900; obituaries in the *Waxahachie Enterprise,* Dec. 27, 1921; Aug. 31, 1925; Jan. 26, 1929; May 29, 1933.

3. Design 438 first appeared in *Shoppell's Modern Houses* 2, no. 1 (Jan. 1887): 18. The same exterior design, but with a floor plan first closer to the one used in the Dunlap House appeared as Design No. 581 in *Shoppell's Modern Houses* 3, no. 3 (Apr. 1889): 63.

4. Barber, *Cottage Souvenir No. 2,* Design No. 56, pp. 118–19. The Powell House no longer exists. It was located on the northwest corner of W. Marvin at Bryson St. (originally named Hiland).

5. Ellis County Mechanic's Liens (Sept. 17, 1892), 1:351.

6. Biographical information on F. P. and Myrtle Powell: U.S. Bureau of the Census, Records for Ellis County, 1880 and 1900; Ellis County Tax Records, 1892 and 1903 (microfilm), Sims Library, Waxahachie, Tex.; wedding announcement, "Powell-Middleton," *Waxahachie Enterprise,* June 3, 1892; Mary Mortimer, "GFWC Shakespeare Club—The First 100 Years," *Waxahachie Daily Light,* Feb. 16, 1997.

7. Biographical information on Ed Williams and family: U.S. Bureau of the Census, Records for Ellis County, 1880 and 1900; *Waxahachie Enterprise,* Jan. 20, Feb. 17, Feb. 24, and Aug. 4, 1893.

8. Will of John G. Williams, Jan. 16, 1893, Ellis County Wills (microfilm), Sims Library, Waxahachie, Tex.

9. Ellis County Mechanic's Liens (Oct. 11, 1893), 1:490–500.

10. Ellis County, County Attorney's Docket, State Cases, nos. 2674, 3091, and 3440, Ellis County Courthouse, Waxahachie, Tex.; Ellis County, Judgment Records (Dec. 12, 1899), 4:105, Ellis County Courthouse, Waxahachie, Tex.; Will of Cynisca Williams, June 3, 1901, Ellis County Wills (microfilm), Sims Library, Waxahachie, Tex.

11. Hosford House, 3209 Highway 77N. The exterior of the house has been significantly altered. Construction date given by Buddy Hosford, descendent of William Hosford in a telephone interview with the author, Apr. 22, 1998.

12. Ellis County Mechanic's Liens (July 16, 1894), 1:583.

13. Biographical information on J. J. Metcalfe and family: U.S. Bureau of the Census, Records for Ellis County, 1880 and 1900; Ellis County Tax Records, 1892 and 1903 (microfilm), Sims Library, Waxahachie, Tex.; *Waxahachie Enterprise,* Jan. 14, 1898; Ellis County Mechanic's Liens (Sept. 17, 1892), 1:351; *Ellis County Mirror,* July 6 and 27, 1905, reprinted in *Ellis County Genealogical Society Records,* vol. 17.

14. Barber, *New Model Dwellings,* Design No. 84, p. 97.

15. George F. Barber, *Appreciation,* unpaged.

16. Ellis County Mechanic's Liens (Nov. 4, 1895).

17. Ellis County History Workshop, *History of Ellis County, Texas,* 57.

18. Biographical information on H. W. Trippet and family: U.S. Bureau of the Census, Records for Ellis County, 1880; *Waxahachie Enterprise,* Apr. 17, 1891, Jan. 25, 1895, and Mar. 6, 1896, Ellis County History Workshop, *History of Ellis County,* 69; *Memorial and Biographical History of Ellis County,* 143; Ellis County Mechanic's Liens (Nov. 4, 1895).

19. *Waxahachie Enterprise,* Jan. 1, Aug. 12, and Dec. 23, 1898; May 19, June 2, July 28, and Sept. 29, 1899; Jan. 19, 1900. Ellis County Tax Records, 1892, 1895, and 1897 (microfilm), Sims Library, Waxahachie, Tex.

20. U.S. Bureau of the Census, Records for Tarrant County, 1900; U.S. Bureau of the Census, Records for Greer County, Okla., 1910.

21. "Residence at Bridgeport, Conn.," *Scientific*

American: Architects' and Builders' Edition 13, no. 5 (May 1892): 66–67 and color plate. Biographical information on M. T. Patrick and family: *Memorial and Biographical History of Ellis County,* reprint ed., 142–43, 674–75; Ellis County History Workshop, *History of Ellis County,* 55, 57; U.S. Bureau of the Census, Records for Ellis County, 1880 and 1900; *Ellis County Genealogical Society Records,* 19:38; *Waxahachie Enterprise,* Feb. 9, 1900, and July 3, 1903; *Waxahachie Daily Light,* July 23, 1930; Oct. 4, 1934; Dec. 2, 1969.

22. Emily Kemble Graham and Anne Graham Allen, interview by Margaret Culbertson, Waxahachie, Tex., May 3, 1997.

23. Ibid.

24. Information on C. J. Griggs and family: U.S. Bureau of the Census, Records for Limestone County, 1880; U.S. Bureau of the Census, Records for Ellis County, 1900; Ellis County Mechanic's Liens, vols. 1–3; Ellis County Tax Records, 1892 (microfilm), Sims Library, Waxahachie, Tex.; Waxahachie city directory, 1907.

Chapter 8. Conclusion

1. Josephine Mason Scrimgeour, "Notes on the Design of a House," ca. 1912, in Morgan Family Papers, Rosenberg Library, Galveston, Tex.

2. Dexter, *Texas: Imperial State,* sections on Waxahachie and Palestine. Trippet House, 209 N. Grand Ave., Waxahachie, based on a design by George F. Barber, see ch. 7. Hufsmith House, 207 Magnolia St., Palestine, Tex., significantly altered: Carl L. Avera, *Wind Swept Land,* 85.

3. Gowans, *Comfortable House,* 63–67.

Bibliography

Aladdin Plan of Industrial Housing. 2d ed. Bay City, Mich.: Aladdin Company, 1920.

Aldrich, Armistead Albert. *History of Houston County, Texas.* San Antonio: Naylor Company, 1943.

Alexander, Drury Blakely. *Texas Homes of the Nineteenth Century.* Austin: University of Texas Press, 1966.

American Architectural Books [microform]. New Haven, Conn.: Research Publications, [1971–72].

American Homes. Knoxville, Tenn. 1895–1904.

Associated Architects. *Fifty House Plans Designed for Home Builders in the Southwest.* Dallas: Associated Architects, 1910.

Austin: Its Architects and Architecture (1836–1986). Austin: Austin Chapter AIA, 1986.

Austin Chapter, American Institute of Architects. *Austin and Its Architecture.* Austin: Austin Chapter AIA, 1976.

Avera, Carl L. *Wind Swept Land.* San Antonio: Naylor Company, 1964.

Bangor (Me.) Daily Whig and Courier. 1867.

Barber, George F. *Appreciation.* [Knoxville, Tenn.: S. B. Newman and Company, 1899].

———. *Art in Architecture.* 2d ed. Knoxville, Tenn.: S. B. Newman and Co., 1902–1903.

———. *Artistic Homes: How to Plan and How to Build Them.* Knoxville, Tenn.: S. B. Newman and Co., 1893.

———. *Cottage Souvenir, Revised and Enlarged.* Knoxville, Tenn.: S. B. Newman and Company, 1892.

———. *Cottage Souvenir No. 2.* Knoxville, Tenn.: S. B. Newman and Company, 1891. Reprint, with introduction by Michael A. Tomlan, Watkins Glen, N.Y.: American Life Foundation, 1982.

———. *Modern Dwellings.* 3d ed. Knoxville, Tenn.: S. B. Newman and Company, 1901.

———. *Modern Dwellings.* 5th ed. Knoxville, Tenn.: Barber and Klutz, Architects, 1905.

———. *New Model Dwellings.* Knoxville, Tenn.: George F. Barber and Company, 1895–96. On microfilm in *American Architectural Books,* reel 5.

Barnes, Lavonia Jenkins. *Early Homes of Waco, and the People Who Lived in Them.* Waco: Texian Press, 1970.

Barnstone, Howard. *The Galveston That Was.* New York: Macmillan Company, 1966.

Beasley, Ellen, and Stephen Fox. *Galveston Architecture Guidebook.* Houston: Rice University Press, 1996.

Beaumont (Tex.) Enterprise. 1889.

Bellville (Tex.) Countryman. 1860.

Benjamin, Asher. *American Builder's Companion.* 6th ed. Boston: R. P. and C. Williams, 1827. Reprint, New York: Dover, 1969.

———. *Architect, or Practical House Carpenter.* Boston: L. Coffin, 1844. Reprint, New York: Dover, 1988.

———. *Practice of Architecture.* Boston: Benjamin B. Mussey, 1839. Reprint, New York: Da Capo Press, 1994.

A Better Day Is Dawning: History of the First One Hundred Years of the First Baptist Church of Bryan, Texas. Austin: Von Boeckmann–Jones, 1966.

Bicknell, A. J., and Company. *Bicknell's Village Builder and Supplement.* New York: A. J. Bicknell and Company, 1878. Reprint, New York: Dover Publications, 1979. Reprint, with an introduction by Paul Goeldner, Watkins Glen, N.Y.: American Life Foundation, 1976.

Biddle, Owen. *Young Carpenter's Assistant.* Philadelphia: Benjamin Johnson, 1805; on microfilm in *American Architectural Books,* reel 11.

Bracken, Dorothy Kendall. *Early Texas Homes.* Dallas: Southern Methodist University Press, 1956.

Bucher, Ward, ed. *Dictionary of Building Preservation.* New York: Preservation Press, J. Wiley, 1996.

Builder and Woodworker. 1880–94.

Bungalowcraft Company. *Homes of the Moment.* Los Angeles: Bungalowcraft Company, 1929.

Bungalow Magazine (Los Angeles, Calif.). 1909–10.

Bungalow Magazine (Seattle, Wash.). 1912–18.

Burkholder, Mary V. *Down the Acequia Madre: In the King William Historic District.* San Antonio: Privately printed, 1976.

———. *The King William Area: A History and Guide to the Houses.* 2d ed. San Antonio: King William Association, 1977.

Campbell, Ida. *Oh, Strange New World.* Austin: Nortex Press, 1986.

Carpentry and Building. 1879–1909.

Chivers, Herbert C. *Artistic Homes.* St. Louis: Herbert C. Chivers, n.d.

Cleaveland, Henry W., et al. *Village and Farm Cottages.* New York: D. Appleton and Company, 1856. Reprint, Watkins Glen, N.Y.: American Life Foundation, 1982.

Comstock, William T. *American Cottages.* N.Y.: W. T. Comstock, 1883. Reprint, titled *Country Houses and Seaside Cottages of the Victorian Era,* New York: Dover, 1989.

———. *Modern Architectural Designs and Details.* N.Y.: W. T. Comstock, 1881. Reprint, titled *Victorian Domestic Architectural Plans and Details,* New York: Dover, 1987.

Country Life in America. 1910.

Craftsman. 1901–16.

Crain Ready-Cut House Company. *Crain Ready-Cut House Company, Catalogue 6.* Houston: Crain Ready-Cut House Company, n.d.

———. *Ready-Cut and Sectional Houses, Catalogue No. 5.* Houston: Crain Ready-Cut House Company, n.d. [circa 1925].

———*Ready-Cut Homes, Catalogue No. 4.* Houston: Crain Ready-Cut House Company, n.d.

Creese, Walter. "Fowler and the Domestic Octagon." *Art Bulletin* 28 (June 1946): 89–102.

Crosbie, Michael J. "From 'Cookbooks' to 'Menus': The Transformation of Architecture Books in Nineteenth-Century America." *Material Culture* 17 (1985): 1–23.

Culbertson, Margaret. "From Mail House to Your House: Catalogue Sources of Houston Domestic Architecture 1880–1930." *Cite: The Architecture and Design Review of Houston* no. 24 (Spring 1990): 22–23.

———. "Mail-Order Mansions: Catalogue Sources of Domestic Architecture in North Central Texas."

Legacies: A History Journal for Dallas and North Central Texas 4, no. 2 (Fall 1992): 8–20.

Culbertson, Margaret, and Ellen Beasley. "Use of Published House Plans for Domestic Architecture in Texas: 1890–1930." Unpublished report submitted to Texas Society of Architects, Austin, 1986.

Curl, James Stevens. *Encyclopaedia of Architectural Terms.* London: Donhead, 1993.

Dallas Morning News. January 20, 1910.

Dexter, W. W. *Texas: Imperial State of America with Her Diadem of Cities.* St. Louis, Mo.: Sam'l F. Myerson Printing Company, 1904.

"Downes-Aldrich House, National Register of Historic Places Inventory-Nomination Form." 1977. Texas Historical Commission, Austin.

Downing, Andrew Jackson. *Architecture of Country Houses.* 1850. Reprint, with an introduction by J. Stewart Johnson, New York: Dover, 1969.

———. *Cottage Residences.* New York: Wiley and Putnam, 1842. Reprint, titled *Victorian Cottage Residences,* New York: Dover Publications, 1981. On microfilm in *American Architectural Books,* reel 24.

Dumbarton Oaks Colloquium on the History of Landscape Architecture (11th). *Prophet with Honor: The Career of Andrew Jackson Downing, 1815–1852.* Washington, D.C.: Dumbarton Oaks Research Library and Collection, 1989.

Ellis County History: The Basic 1882 Book (With the Presidents Section Deleted): With Additional Biographies. Waxahachie, Tex.: Ellis County Historical Museum and Art Gallery, 1972.

Ellis County History Workshop. *History of Ellis County, Texas.* Waco: Texian Press, 1972.

Ellis County Mechanic's Liens. Volumes 1–4, 7.

Endangered Historic Properties of Texas. Austin: Texas Historical Commission, 1989.

Fall, Mrs. Henry, ed. *The Key to the City of Houston.* Houston: State Printing Company, 1908.

Farm and Ranch. 1901.

Fowler, Orson Squire. *A Home for All.* 1853. Reprint, titled *The Octagon House: A Home for All,* New York: Dover Publications, 1973.

Fox, Stephen. *Houston Architectural Guide.* Houston: American Institute of Architects, Houston Chapter, 1990.

French, Gery E. "Letters: Palliser Pedigree." *Old-House Journal* 19, no. 4 (July–August 1991): 8, 10.

Galveston Evening Standard. April 2, 1887.

Galveston Weekly News. March 8, 1859.

Garnsey, George O. *American Glossary of Architectural Terms.* Chicago: Clark and Langley Company, 1887. On microfilm in *American Architectural Books,* reel 37.

Garvin, James L. "Mail-Order House Plans and American Victorian Architecture." *Winterthur Portfolio* 16, no. 4 (1981): 309–34.

Goebel, Nancy. "Historic Homes." *Texas Homes* 9, no. 1 (January 1985): 73–83.

———. "Pluck of the Irish." *Texas Homes* 9, no. 7 (July 1985): 51–53.

Gottfried, Herbert, and Jan Jennings. *American Vernacular Design: 1870–1940.* Ames: Iowa State University Press, 1988.

Gowans, Alan. *The Comfortable House: North American Suburban Architecture, 1890–1930.* Cambridge, Mass.: MIT Press, 1986.

Graham, Emily Kemble, and Anne Graham Allen. Interview by Margaret Culbertson, Waxahachie, Texas, May 3, 1997.

A Guide to the Older Neighborhoods of Dallas. Dallas: Historic Preservation League, 1986.

Gulf Coast Lumberman. 1913–22.

Guter, Robert P., and Janet W. Foster. *Building by the Book: Pattern-Book Architecture in New Jersey.* New Brunswick, N.J.: Rutgers University Press, 1992.

Hafertepe, Kenneth. *Abner Cook: Master Builder on the Texas Frontier.* Austin: Texas State Historical Association, 1992.

———. *History of Ashton Villa.* Austin: Texas State Historical Association, 1991.

Hamblett, Gus. "The 'Plain Style:' Some Sources for the Greek Revival in Texas." *Texas Architect* 36, no. 3 (May–June 1986): 60–69.

Hause, Burt, and Jeanne Hause. *The Interview* [by Kathleen Jones Alexander]. Beeville, Tex.: Privately printed, 1985.

Haviland, John. *Builder's Assistant.* 2d ed. Baltimore, Md.: Fielding Lucas, Jr., [1830].

Henderson County Historical Commission. *Old Homes of Henderson County.* Crockett: Publications Development Company, 1982.

Henry, Jay C. *Architecture in Texas, 1895–1945.* Austin: University of Texas Press, 1993.

"Heritage Homes" (calendar). Brownwood, Tex.: Southwest State Bank, 1979.

Hersey, George L. "Godey's Choice." *Journal of the Society of Architectural Historians* 18, no. 3 (October 1959): 104–11.

Historic American Buildings: Texas. 2 vols. New York: Garland Publishing, Inc., 1979.

Historic American Buildings Survey [microform]. Cambridge, England: Chadwyck-Healey, 1980.

Historic Preservation Council for Tarrant County. *Tarrant County Historic Resources Survey: Fort Worth: Upper North, Northeast, East, Far South, and Far West.* Fort Worth: Historic Preservation Council for Tarrant County, 1989.

———. *Tarrant County Historic Resources Survey: Phase III, Fort Worth's Southside.* Fort Worth: Historic Preservation Council for Tarrant County, 1986.

Hite-Smith, Charles. "Plans and Plan-Making." *American Homes* 2, no. 1 (January 1896): 22–25.

Hobbs, Isaac. *Hobbs's Architecture.* Philadelphia: J. B. Lippincott, 1873. Rev. ed., 1876.

Hodgson, Frederick T. *Practical Bungalows and Cottages for Town and Country.* Chicago: Frederick J. Drake and Company, 1906.

Holland's Magazine. 1905–23.

Holman, E. E. *A Book of Bungalows.* Philadelphia: E. E. Holman, 1906.

Homes (Houston). 1911–12.

Homes of the Moment. Los Angeles: Bungalowcraft Company, 1929.

Hopkins, David S. *Houses and Cottages.* Grand Rapids, Mich.: D. S. Hopkins, 1889. On microfilm in *American Architectural Books,* reel 45.

Houghton, Dorothy Knox Howe, et al. *Houston's Forgotten Heritage.* Houston: Rice University Press, 1991.

Houston Daily Post. 1911.

Hussey, E. C. *Home Building.* New York: E. C. Hussey, 1875. Reprint, titled *Victorian Home Building,* Watkins Glen, N.Y.: American Life Foundation, 1976.

Inland Architect. 1887–88.

Jennings, Jan. "Leila Ross Wilburn: Plan-Book Architect." *Women's Art Journal* 10 (Spring–Summer 1989): 10–16.

Johnston, Annie F. *Mary Ware in Texas.* Boston: L. C. Page, 1910.

Keith's Magazine on Homebuilding. 1899–1925.

King, Anthony. *The Bungalow: The Production of a Global Culture.* 2d ed. New York: Oxford University Press, 1995.

Knoxville (Tenn.) Journal and Tribune. 1915.

Ladies' Home Journal. 1901, 1910.

Lafever, Minard. *Beauties of Modern Architecture*. New York: D. Appleton and Company, 1835. Reprint, New York: Da Capo Press, 1968.

———. *Modern Builder's Guide*. New York: Henry C. Sleight, Collins and Hannay, 1833. Reprint, New York: Dover Publications, 1969.

Lancaster, Clay. *The American Bungalow, 1880–1920*. New York: Abbeville Press, 1985.

———. "Builders' Guide and Plan Books and American Architecture." *Magazine of Art* 61 (January 1948): 16–22.

McAlester, Virginia, and Lee McAlester. *Field Guide to American Houses*. New York: Knopf, 1984.

McDonald, William Lloyd. *Dallas Rediscovered: A Photographic Chronicle of Urban Expansion 1870–1925*. Dallas: Dallas Historical Society, 1978.

McMurry, Sally. *Families and Farmhouses in Nineteenth-Century America*. New York: Oxford University Press, 1988.

Map of Houston Heights. N.d.

Maxson, Peter Flagg. "The Octagon Option in Texas." *Perspective* 9 (December 1980): 14–17.

Memorial and Biographical History of Ellis County. Chicago: Lewis Publishing Company, 1892.

Montgomery, Linda. "Calvert." *Texas Homes* 4, no. 2 (March 1980): 83.

Moore, Harvin C. "The Restoration of the Nichols-Rice House." *AIA Journal* (January 1962): 28.

Mott, Frank L. *History of American Magazines, 1741–1850*. Cambridge, Mass.: Harvard University Press, 1938.

National Builder. 1885–1924.

Navarro County Mechanic's Liens. Volumes 4 and 7. Navarro County Courthouse, Corsicana, Texas.

Ochsner, Jeffrey Karl, ed. *Shaping Seattle Architecture*. Seattle: University of Washington Press, 1994.

Old Homes of Houston County, Texas. Crockett, Tex.: Publications Development Company, 1983.

Page, Henry A. "Design for an Octagon House." *Horticulturist* 4, no. 11 (May 1850): 516–18 and frontispiece.

Palliser, George. *Palliser's American Cottage Homes*. Bridgeport, Conn.: George Palliser, 1876. Reprint, titled *George Palliser's Model Homes for the People*, Watkins Glen, N.Y.: American Life Foundation, 1978.

Palliser, Palliser and Company. *Palliser's American Architecture*. New York: Palliser, Palliser and Company, 1888. Reprint, Watkins Glen, N.Y.: American Life Foundation, 1978.

———. *Palliser's American Cottage Homes*. Bridgeport, Conn.: Palliser, Palliser and Company, [1878].

———. *Palliser's Late Victorian Architecture: A Facsimile of George and Charles Palliser's Model Homes (1878) and American Cottage Homes (1878), as Republished in 1888 under the Title American Architecture, and New Cottage Homes and Details (1887)*. Watkins Glen, N.Y.: American Life Foundation, 1978.

———. *Palliser's Model Homes*. Bridgeport, Conn.: Palliser, Palliser and Company, 1878.

Patoski, Joe Nick. "Houses by Number." *Domain: The Lifestyle Magazine of Texas Monthly* (Summer 1988): 20–24.

Patterson, Bessie. *History of Deaf Smith County, Featuring Pioneer Families*. Hereford, Tex.: Pioneer Publishers, 1964.

Poore, Patricia. "The Bungalow and Why We Love It So." *Old-House Journal* 13, no. 4 (May 1985): 90–93.

———. "Pattern Book Architecture." *Old-House Journal* 7, no. 12 (December 1980): 183: 190–93.

Portals at the Pass: El Paso Area Architecture to 1930. El Paso: El Paso Chapter, American Institute of Architects, 1984.

"Preview of a Post-war Prefabricated Home." *Prefabricated Homes* 3, no. 5 (September 1944): 8–11, 24.

Reiff, Daniel D. "Identifying Mail-Order and Catalog Houses." *Old-House Journal* 23, no. 5 (September–October 1995): 30–37.

Ridgway, Susan M. "Old-House Living In Central Texas." *Old-House Journal* 10, no. 11 (November 1982): 223–26.

Roark, Carol. *Fort Worth's Legendary Landmarks*. Fort Worth: Texas Christian University Press, 1995.

Robinson, Willard B. *Gone from Texas: Our Lost Architectural Heritage*. College Station: Texas A&M University Press, 1981.

Ruff, Ann. *Historic Homes of Texas*. Houston: Lone Star Books, 1987.

San Antonio Chapter, American Institute of Architects. *Guide to San Antonio Architecture*. San Antonio: San Antonio Chapter AIA, 1986.

San Antonio Light. 1909–10, 1915, 1921.

Sasser, Elizabeth Skidmore. *Dugout to Deco: Building in West Texas, 1880–1930*. Lubbock: Texas Tech University Press, 1993.

Scardino, Barrie. "The Development of Domestic Architecture." In *Houston's Forgotten Heritage*, by Dorothy Knox Howe Houghton, et al. Houston: Rice University Press, 1991.

Schuyler, David. *Apostle of Taste: Andrew Jackson*

Downing, 1815–1852. Baltimore, Md.: Johns Hopkins University Press, 1996.

Schweitzer, Robert, and Michael W. R. Davis. *America's Favorite Homes: Mail-Order Catalogues as a Guide to Popular Early-Twentieth-Century Houses.* Detroit, Mich.: Wayne State University Press, 1990.

Scientific American, Architects' and Builders' Edition. 1885–94.

Scientific American, Building Edition. 1895–1901.

Scientific American, Building Monthly. 1902–1905.

Scrimgeour, Josephine Mason. "Notes on the Design of a House," circa 1912. In Morgan Family Papers, Rosenberg Library, Galveston, Texas.

Sears, Roebuck and Company. *Book of Modern Homes.* Chicago: Sears, Roebuck and Company, 1911.

———. *Modern Homes.* Chicago: Sears, Roebuck and Company, 1914.

———. *Sears, Roebuck Catalog of Houses, 1926: An Unabridged Reprint.* New York: Dover, 1991.

Shoppell, Robert W., comp. *Modern Houses, Beautiful Homes.* New York: Co-operative Building Plan Association, [1887].

Shoppell's Modern Houses. 1886–1904.

Sister Mary Agatha. *History of Houston Heights, 1891–1918.* Houston: Premier Printing Company, 1956.

Sloan, Samuel. *Model Architect.* Philadelphia: E. S. Jones, 1852. Reprint, titled *Sloan's Victorian Buildings,* New York: Dover Publications, 1980.

Smith County Mechanic's Liens. Volume 4.

Standard Building Investment Company. *Standard Bungalows.* Los Angeles: Standard Building Investment Company, 1913.

"Stark House, 611 W. Green, Orange. Application Form for Official Texas Historical Marker." November 1, 1975. Nelda C. and H. J. Lutcher Stark Foundation, Orange, Texas.

Steely, James Wright. *A Catalog of Texas Properties in the National Register of Historic Places.* Austin: Texas Historical Commission, 1984.

Steidle, Harry H. "A Statement from the Prefabricated Home Manufacturers Association." *Arts + Architecture* 61, no. 7 (July 1944): 41–42.

Stevenson, Katherine Cole, and H. Ward Jandl. *Houses by Mail: A Guide to Houses from Sears, Roebuck and Company.* Washington, D.C.: Preservation Press, 1986.

Stickley, Gustav. *More Craftsman Homes.* New York: Craftsman Publishing, 1912. Reprint, New York: Dover Publications, 1982.

Stillwell, E. W. *Representative California Homes.* Los Angeles: E. W. Stillwell and Company, n.d.

———. *West Coast Bungalows.* Los Angeles: E. W. Stillwell and Company, n.d.

Suburbanite (Houston). 1908.

Sweeting, Adam W. *Reading Houses and Building Books: Andrew Jackson Downing and the Architecture of Popular Literature, 1835–1855.* Hanover, N.H.: University Press of New England, 1996.

Tatman, Sandra L. *Biographical Dictionary of Philadelphia Architects, 1700–1930.* Boston: G. K. Hall, 1985.

Telling, George P. *Telling Plan Book: Spanish and Italian Bungalows.* Pasadena, Calif.: George P. Telling, n.d.

Texas General Contractors Association. *TGCA Monthly Bulletin.* 1924–25, 1928.

Tomlan, Michael A. "The Palliser Brothers and Their Publications." In *Palliser's Late Victorian Architecture,* by Palliser, Palliser and Co. Reprint ed. Watkins Glen, N.Y.: American Life Foundation, 1978.

——— "Popular and Professional American Architectural Literature in the Late Nineteenth Century." Ph.D. dissertation, Cornell University, 1983.

Turner, Drexel, et al. *Houston Architectural Survey.* 6 vols. Houston: n.p., 1980–81.

Turner, Martha Anne. *Old Nacogdoches in the Jazz Age.* Austin, Tex.: Madrona Press, 1976.

Tyler, Ron, ed. *New Handbook of Texas.* Austin: Texas Historical Association, 1996.

Upton, Dell. "Pattern Books and Professionalism." *Winterthur Portfolio* 19, nos. 2–3 (1984): 107–50.

U.S. Bureau of the Census. Records, 1880, 1900, 1910, 1920.

Utley, Dan K. ed., *Sentimental Journey: A Guide to Preserving the Architectural Heritage of Georgetown, Texas.* Georgetown, Tex.: Georgetown Heritage Society, 1988.

Waxahachie Daily News.

Waxahachie Enterprise.

"Weatherford." *Texas Homes* 6, no. 3 (April 1982): 28.

Wilkinson, Jeff. "Who They Were: Geo. Palliser." *Old-House Journal* 18, no. 6 (November–December 1990): 18, 20.

Williams, T. J. *Better Built Homes for Less Money.* Houston: T. J. Williams House Manufacturing Company, [1915].

Williamson, Roxanne Kuter. *Austin, Texas: An American Architectural History.* San Antonio: Trinity University Press, 1973.

Wilson, Henry L. *The Bungalow Book.* 4th ed. Los Angeles: Henry L. Wilson, 1908.

Winter, Robert. *The California Bungalow.* Los Angeles: Hennessey and Ingalls, 1980.

Wofford, Vera Dean. *Hale County: Facts and Folklore.* Lubbock, Tex.: Pica Publishing Company, 1978.

Woodland Heights. Houston: William A. Wilson Realty Company, 1910.

Woodward, George E. *Woodward's Country Homes.* New York: Geo. E. Woodward, 1865. Reprint. Watkins Glen, N.Y.: American Life Foundation, n.d.

———. *Woodward's National Architect.* New York: Geo. E. Woodward, 1869. Reprint, titled *A Victorian Housebuilder's Guide,* New York: Dover, 1988.

Wright, Gwendolyn. *Moralism and the Model Home.* Chicago: University of Chicago Press, 1980.

Ye Planry Beautiful Homes. Dallas: Ye Planry Company, 1914.

Ye Planry Bungalows. Los Angeles: Ye Planry Company, 1908.

Yoho, Jud. *Craftsman Bungalows.* Seattle, Wash.: Jud Yoho, 1916.

Ziegler, Jesse A. *Wave of the Gulf.* San Antonio: Naylor Company, 1938.

Index

Pages containing illustrations appear in italics.